About This Book

Why is this topic important?

Organizational consulting generally has a broader focus than training. Whereas a trainer might develop peoples' understanding of team roles, a consultant might help a dysfunctional team function. Similarly, a trainer might deliver a workshop on developing good time management and productivity skills, whereas a consultant might be contracted to analyze and reorganize workflow through a team or through an entire division or operating unit. There are clearly similarities between training and consulting—and the terms are often used interchangeably—but each has a unique focus and requires divergent approaches, tools, and techniques.

What can you achieve with this book?

Offering entirely new content each year, the consulting edition of *The Pfeiffer Annual* showcases the latest thinking and cutting-edge approaches to organization development and performance improvement contributed by practicing consultants, organizational systems experts, and academics. Designed for both the dedicated consultant and the training professional who straddles both roles, the *Annual* represents a unique source of new knowledge and ideas, as well as practical and proven applications for facilitating better work processes, implementing and sustaining change, and improving organizational effectiveness.

How is this book organized?

The book is divided into four sections: Experiential Learning Activities (ELAs), Editor's Choice, Inventories, Questionnaires, and Surveys, and Articles and Discussion Resources. The materials can be freely reproduced for use in the normal course of an assignment. ELAs are the mainstay of the *Annual* and cover a broad range of consulting topics. The activities are presented as complete and ready-to-use designs for working with groups; facilitator instructions and all necessary hand-outs and participant materials are included. Editor's Choice pieces allow us to select material that doesn't fit the other categories and take advantage of "hot topics." The instrument section introduces proven survey and assessment tools for gathering and sharing data on some aspect of performance. The articles section presents the best current thinking about workplace performance and organization development. Use these for your own professional enrichment or as resources for working with others.

About Pfeiffer

Pfeiffer serves the professional development and hands-on resource needs of training and human resource practitioners and gives them products to do their jobs better. We deliver proven ideas and solutions from experts in HR development and HR management, and we offer effective and customizable tools to improve workplace performance. From novice to seasoned professional, Pfeiffer is the source you can trust to make yourself and your organization more successful.

Essential Knowledge Pfeiffer produces insightful, practical, and comprehensive materials on topics that matter the most to training and HR professionals. Our Essential Knowledge resources translate the expertise of seasoned professionals into practical, how-to guidance on critical workplace issues and problems. These resources are supported by case studies, worksheets, and job aids and are frequently supplemented with CD-ROMs, websites, and other means of making the content easier to read, understand, and use.

Essential Tools Pfeiffer's Essential Tools resources save time and expense by offering proven, ready-to-use materials—including exercises, activities, games, instruments, and assessments—for use during a training or team-learning event. These resources are frequently offered in looseleaf or CD-ROM format to facilitate copying and customization of the material.

Pfeiffer also recognizes the remarkable power of new technologies in expanding the reach and effectiveness of training. While e-hype has often created whizbang solutions in search of a problem, we are dedicated to bringing convenience and enhancements to proven training solutions. All our e-tools comply with rigorous functionality standards. The most appropriate technology wrapped around essential content yields the perfect solution for today's on-the-go trainers and human resource professionals.

Pfeiffer
www.pfeiffer.com

Essential resources for training and HR professionals

Call for Papers

How would you like to be published in the *Pfeiffer Annuals*? Possible topics for submissions include group and team building, organization development, leadership, problem solving, presentation and communication skills, consulting and facilitation, and training-the-trainer. Contributions may be in one of the following three formats:

- Experiential Learning Activities

- Inventories, Questionnaires, and Surveys

- Articles and Discussion Resources

To receive a copy of the submission packet, which explains the requirements and will help you determine format, language, and style to use, contact *Annual* editor Elaine Biech at Pfeifferannual@aol.com or by calling 757–588–3939.

Elaine Biech, EDITOR

The *2004*
Pfeiffer
ANNUAL

CONSULTING

Pfeiffer
A Wiley Imprint
www.pfeiffer.com

Printed in the United States of America

ISBN: 0-7879-6929-X
ISSN: 1046-333X

Acquiring Editor: Martin Delahoussaye
Director of Development: Kathleen Dolan Davies
Developmental Editor: Susan Rachmeler
Editor: Rebecca Taff
Senior Production Editor: Dawn Kilgore
Manufacturing Supervisor: Bill Matherly
Interior Design: Chris Wallace
Cover Design: Chris Wallace
Illustrations: Leigh McLellan Design

Printed in the United States of America

Printing 10 9 8 7 6 5 4 3 2 1

Preface

Fitness from the Inside Out

Is it just a coincidence or is there a movement afoot in which many of us are reexamining who we are, what our purpose in life is, and how we are spending our precious moments on earth? Is it a coincidence that *The Purpose-Driven Life* by Rick Warren has been on the bestseller list for almost a year and that *Self Matters* by Phillip McGraw hit the bestseller list (landing in the top ten) its first week in release? Is it a coincidence that I recently moderated a keynote panel for ASTD's International Conference where each of the five panelists, all best-selling authors, commented on the higher purpose of their profession? Is it a coincidence that Dr. Wayne Dyer's book, *10 Secrets for Success and Inner Peace*, continues to find top placement in major bookstores after three years?

Indeed, many of us are trying to find answers to "Who am I?" "What is my purpose?" "How can I balance my time wisely?" Therefore, is it any wonder that many of the submissions for the *2004 Pfeiffer Annuals* were built around this very theme? A coincidence? Probably not. Many of us are questioning who we are, what we do, how we do it, and even where and when we do it. It seems that we are looking for answers inside to be better on the outside. I refer to this self-examination as "fitness from the inside out." Both volumes have this theme running through them. I think you will find it refreshingly personal, yet powerfully professional. Let me share some of these highlights from both the Training and the Consulting *Annuals* with you.

The Training *Annual*, for example has three ELAs that reflect this personal examination. "Quotations: Reflecting on Others' Experiences" allows participants to reflect and find personal meaning in others' experiences. "Highly Leveraged Moments: Enhancing the Quality of Internal Life in the Workplace" gives participants an opportunity to connect with meaningful moments while shifting perspective. "Zen with a Sense of Humor" is perfect for opening a session where you want to ease participants into the self-improvement mode in a light-hearted way. Do read the "Z-Biz" article. The author uses corporate examples to introduce a concept of creating open, value expressive, equitable environments that allow the core of the individual to remain intact no matter what is happening in the organization.

The Editor's Choice section is new this year and showcases another activity, "Value Enhancement: Adding Value to Your Work," related to fitness from the inside out. Research shows that employees who are most satisfied with their jobs are those who believe they are contributing to the organization. This submission was chosen for the Editor's Choice section primarily because of its importance to the workplace and to the individuals who do the work.

The Consulting *Annual* also has a representative sample of submissions related to "fitness from the inside out." Start by reading "Life-Centering Stories," which explains a process that the author uses in personal coaching sessions to explore life-centering moments that form a template of perception and responses used by individuals. This is truly an inspirational work. There are at least four ELAs you may wish to explore in this volume. The first is "Z Fantasy" by the same author who wrote "Z-Biz" in the Training volume. She introduces you to the fine art of haiku. "Hubris: Eliminating the Personal Delusion of Arrogance" explores a key leadership pitfall that could be inherent in all of us. "Career Choices: Building Self-Knowledge" explores the role that values play in both personal career development and the culture of various work environments. And last, "Diversity from Within" is a great addition to your diversity training or one-on-one coaching. Finally, you may wish to read "Change the Snapshot: Change Perceptions" to assist your clients to fully understand how perceptions become reality and how difficult they are to change. And "fitness from the inside out" will often depend on changing perceptions.

Coincidental? No, I don't view this as coincidental. I do believe your participants and clients are looking for more opportunities to grow from the inside out. I believe many of you are as well. Both the Training and the Consulting *Annuals* have resources to help you do just that.

What Are the Annuals?

The 2004 Pfeiffer Annuals present a collection of practical materials written for trainers, consultants, and performance-improvement technologists. This source for experiential learning activities, resource for instruments, and reference for cutting-edge articles has inspired human resource development (HRD) professionals for thirty-two years.

The *Annuals* are published as a set of two: Training and Consulting. Materials in the training volume focus on skill building and knowledge enhancement. The training volume also features articles that enhance the skills and professional development of trainers. Materials in the consulting volume focus on intervention techniques and organizational systems. The consulting volume also features articles that enhance the skills and professional development of consultants.

Whether you are a trainer, a consultant, a facilitator, or a bit of each, you will find tools and techniques between the *Annual* covers. Trainers, are you looking for ideas to train members of a new department? Design a new training program? Refresh training that is a mainstay in your organization? Incorporate e-learning into your programs? Check out the training volume. Consultants, are you searching for just the right team-building intervention? New concepts for coaching executives? Resources to send to your clients? A new approach to address communication? You will find it in the consulting volume. Facilitators, are you seeking evaluation tools for teams? Feedback tools? Experiential activities to enhance learning? You will find answers in both volumes.

Both volumes provide you with the basics, such as conflict management and communication skills. Both volumes challenge you to use new techniques and models such as storytelling and partnering with your clients. Both volumes show you how to utilize technology, such as evaluating your organization's readiness for web-based learning and online communication, throughout your efforts. And both volumes introduce cutting-edge topics such as using life-centering stories and retaining high-performance employees.

As you might expect, there is some overlap between the two volumes. Therefore, it is sometimes difficult for an editor to determine which volume is the better location for each submission. And indeed, often submissions could be placed in either. As you search for resources, examine both volumes to find materials that will best meet your needs. You will find that, with a slight modification, you will be able to use activities, articles, and instruments from both volumes.

What's New?

If you have used the *Annuals* in the past, you will notice many improvements this year. We hope that the new cover design and the packaging create a look that is both pleasant and practical. The added CD-ROM ensures ease of creating materials for your use. The ELAs have several added features. First, we have added an Activity Summary at the beginning of each activity to provide you with an overview of what to expect. This should save you time in identifying an appropriate ELA. The new reference grid (found in the section introduction) will also assist you as you make your choices. At your request, we have added a "risk rating" to each ELA. The rating will give you a general idea of the level of expertise you should have to conduct the activity. It also provides you with an idea of how much risk is involved that the activity may bomb or get out of hand. We would appreciate feedback from each of you about these new features.

To ensure that you continue to have ideas and materials at your fingertips, be sure that you have a *Reference Guide* to help you identify all the materials available to you.

The *Reference Guide* is a giant index to all of the *Annuals* and the *Handbook of Structured Experiences,* Volumes I through X, that helps you locate just what you need based on topics and key words. A print version of the *Reference Guide* is available for volumes through 1999. An online supplement covering the years through 2003 can be found at www.pfeiffer.com/go/supplement.

Why Are the Annuals So Successful?

There are good reasons that the *Annual* series has been around for over thirty years. In addition to the wide variety of topics and implementation levels, the *Annuals* provide materials that are applicable to varying circumstances. You will find instruments for individuals, teams, and organizations; experiential learning activities to round out workshops, team building, or consulting assignments; and articles to assign as pre-reading, to read to increase your own knowledge base, or to use as reference materials in your writing tasks.

Probably the most important reason the *Annuals* are a success is that they are immediately ready to use. All of the materials in the *Annuals* may be duplicated for educational and training purposes. If you need to adapt or modify the materials to tailor them for your audience's needs, go right ahead. We only request that the credit statement found on the copyright page (and on each reproducible page) be retained on all copies. In addition, if you intend to reproduce the materials in publications for sale or if you wish to use the materials on a large-scale basis (more than one hundred copies in one year), please contact us for prior written permission. Our liberal copyright policy makes it easy and fast for you to use the materials to do your job. Please call us if you have any questions.

Although the *2004 Annuals* are the newest in the series, you will benefit from having the entire series for your use. The *Pfeiffer Library* is available on CD-ROM. I personally refer to many of my *Annuals* from the 1980s. They include several classic activities that have become a mainstay in my team-building designs.

But most of all, the *Annuals* have been a valuable resource for over thirty years because the materials come from professionals like you who work in the field as trainers, consultants, facilitators, educators, and performance-improvement technologists. This ensures that the materials have been tried and perfected in real-life settings with actual participants and clients to meet real-world needs. To this end, we encourage you to submit materials to be considered for publication in the *Annual.* At your request, we will provide a copy of the guidelines for preparing your materials. We are interested in receiving experiential learning activities (group learning activities based on the five stages of the experiential learning cycle: experiencing, publishing, processing, generalizing, and applying); inventories, questionnaires, and surveys (both paper-and-pencil as well as electronic rating scales); and articles and discussion resources (articles that may include theory related to practical application). Contact the Pfeiffer Editorial Department at the address listed on the copyright page for copies of our guidelines for contributors or contact me directly at Box 8249, Norfolk, VA 23503, or by email at pfeifferannual@aol.com. We welcome your comments, ideas, and contributions.

Acknowledgments

Thank you to the dedicated, friendly, thoughtful people at Pfeiffer who produced the 2004 *Annuals*: Kathleen Dolan Davies, Martin Delahoussaye, Dawn Kilgore, Susan Rachmeler, Laura Reizman, and Rebecca Taff. Thank you to Dan of ebb associates inc, who jumped in at the last minute to keep things flowing.

Most important, thank you to our authors, who have once again shared their ideas, techniques, and materials so that HRD professionals everywhere may benefit.

Elaine Biech
Editor
June 2003

The Difference Between Training and Consulting
Which Annual to Use?

The two volumes of the *Pfeiffer Annuals*—training and consulting—are resources for two different but closely related professions. Each *Annual* serves as a collection of tools and support materials used by the professionals in their respective arenas. The volumes include activities, articles, and instruments used by individuals in the training and consulting fields. The training volume is written with the trainer in mind, and the consulting volume is written with the consultant in mind.

How can you differentiate between the two volumes? Let's begin by defining each profession. A *trainer* can be defined as anyone who is responsible for designing and delivering knowledge to adult learners and may include an internal HRD professional employed by an organization or an external practitioner who contracts with an organization to design and conduct training programs. Generally, the trainer is a subject-matter expert who is expected to transfer knowledge so that the trainee can know or do something new. A *consultant* is someone who provides unique assistance or advice (based on what the consultant knows or has experienced) to someone else, usually known as "the client." The consultant may not necessarily be a subject-matter expert in all situations. Often the consultant is an expert at using specific tools to extract, co-ordinate, resolve, organize, expedite, or implement an organizational situation.

The lines between the consulting and training professions have blurred in the past few years. First, the names and titles have blurred. For example, some external trainers call themselves "training consultants" as a way of distinguishing themselves from internal trainers and some organizations now have internal consultants who usually reside in the training department.

Second, the roles have blurred. While a consultant has always been expected to deliver measurable results, now trainers are expected to do so as well. Both are expected to improve performance; both are expected to contribute to the bottom line. Facilitation was at one time thought to be a consultant skill; today trainers are expected to use facilitation skills to train. Training one-on-one was a trainer skill; today consultants train executives one-on-one and call it "coaching."

The introduction of the "performance technologist," whose role is one of combined trainer and consultant, is a perfect example of a new profession that has evolved due to the need for trainers to use more "consulting" techniques in their work. The "performance consultant" is a new role supported by the American Society for Training and Development (ASTD) as it has shifted its focus from training to performance improvement.

As you can see, the roles and goals of training and consulting are not nearly as specific as they once may have been. However, when you step back and examine the two professions from a big-picture perspective, you can more easily differentiate between the two. Maintaining a big-picture focus will also help you determine which *Pfeiffer Annual* to turn to as your first resource.

Both volumes cover the same general topics: communication, teamwork, problem solving, and leadership. However, depending on your requirement and purpose—a training or consulting need—you will use each in different situations. You will select the *Annual* based on *how you will interact with the topic, not on what the topic might be.* Let's take a topic such as teamwork, for example. If you are searching for a lecturette that teaches the advantages of teamwork, a workshop activity that demonstrates the skill of making decisions in a team, or a handout that discusses team stages, look to the Training *Annual.* On the other hand, if you are conducting a team-building session for a dysfunctional team, helping to form a new team, or trying to understand the dynamics of an executive team, you will look to the Consulting *Annual.*

The Training *Annual*

The materials in the Training volume focus on skill building and knowledge enhancement as well as on the professional development of trainers. They generally focus on controlled events: a training program, a conference presentation, a classroom setting.

Look to the Training *Annual* to find ways to improve a training session for 10 to 1,000 people and anything else that falls in the human resource development category:

- Specific experiential learning activities that can be built into a training program;

- Techniques to improve training: debriefing exercises, conducting role plays, managing time;

- Topical lecturettes;

- Ideas to improve a boring training program;

- Icebreakers and energizers for a training session;

- Surveys that can be used in a classroom;

- Ideas for moving an organization from training to performance; and

- Ways to improve your skills as a trainer.

The Consulting *Annual*

The materials in the Consulting volume focus on intervention techniques and organizational systems as well as on the professional development of consultants. They generally focus on "tools" that you can have available just in case: concepts about organizations and their development (or demise) and about more global situations.

Look to the Consulting *Annual* to find ways to improve consulting activities from team building and executive coaching to organization development and strategic planning:

- Skills for working with executives;

- Techniques for solving problems, effecting change, and gathering data;

- Team-building tools, techniques, and tactics;

- Facilitation ideas and methods;

- Processes to examine for improving an organization's effectiveness;

- Surveys that can be used organizationally; and

- Ways to improve your effectiveness as a consultant.

Summary

Even though the professions and the work are closely related and at times interchangeable, there is a difference. Use the following table to help you determine which *Annual* you should scan first for help. Remember, however, that there is some blending of the two and either *Annual* may have your answer. It depends . . .

Element	Training	Consulting
Topics	Teams, Communication, Problem Solving	Teams, Communication, Problem Solving
Topic Focus	Individual, Department	Corporate, Global
Purpose	Skill Building, Knowledge Transfer	Coaching, Strategic Planning, Building Teams
Recipient	Individuals, Departments	Usually More Organizational
Organizational Level	All Workforce Members	Usually Closer to the Top
Delivery Profile	Workshops, Presentations	Intervention, Implementation
Atmosphere	Structured	Unstructured
Time Frame	Defined	Undefined
Organizational Cost	Moderate	High
Change Effort	Low to Moderate	Moderate to High
Setting	Usually a Classroom	Anywhere
Professional Experience	Entry Level, Novice	Proficient, Master Level
Risk Level	Low	High
Professional Needs	Activities, Resources	Tools, Theory
Application	Individual Skills	Usually Organizational System

When you get right down to it, we are all both trainers and consultants. The skills may cross over. A great trainer is also a skilled consultant. And a great consultant is also a skilled trainer. The topics may be the same, but how you implement them may be vastly different. Which *Annual* to use? Remember to think about your purpose in terms of the big picture: consulting or training.

As you can see, we have both covered.

Elaine Biech

Contents

Experiential Learning Activities

Editor's Choice

Inventories, Questionnaires, and Surveys

**Topic is "cutting edge."

Articles and Discussion Resources

Introduction
to The 2004 Pfeiffer Annual: Consulting

Getting the Most from This Resource

The 2004 Pfeiffer Annual: Consulting is the forty-third volume in the *Annual* series, a collection of practical and useful materials for professionals in the broad area described as human resource development (HRD). The materials are written by and for professionals, including trainers, organization-development and organization-effectiveness consultants, performance-improvement technologists, facilitators, educators, instructional designers, and others.

Each *Annual* has three main sections: experiential learning activities; inventories, questionnaires, and surveys; and articles and discussion resources. A fourth section, editor's choice, has been reserved for those unique contributions that do not fit neatly into one of the three main sections, but are valuable as identified by the editorial staff. Each published submission is classified in one of the following categories: Individual Development, Communication, Problem Solving, Groups, Teams, Consulting, Facilitating, Leadership, and Organizations. Within each category, pieces are further classified into logical subcategories, which are identified in the introductions to the three sections.

"Cutting edge" topics are identified in each *Annual*. This designation highlights topics that present information, concepts, tools, or perspectives that may be recent additions to the profession or that have not previously appeared in the *Annual* or are currently "hot topics."

The series continues to provide an opportunity for HRD professionals who wish to share their experiences, their viewpoints, and their processes with their colleagues. To that end, Pfeiffer publishes guidelines for potential authors. These guidelines are available from the Pfeiffer Editorial Department at Jossey-Bass, Inc., in San Francisco, California.

Materials are selected for the *Annuals* based on the quality of the ideas, applicability to real-world concerns, relevance to current HRD issues, clarity of presentation, and ability to enhance our readers' professional development. In addition, we choose experiential learning activities that will create a high degree of enthusiasm among the participants and add enjoyment to the learning process. As in the past several years, the contents of each *Annual* span a wide range of subject matter, reflecting the range of interests of our readers.

Our contributor list includes a wide selection of experts in the field: in-house practitioners, consultants, and academically based professionals. A list of contributors to the *Annual* can be found at the end of the volume, including their names, affiliations, addresses, telephone numbers, facsimile numbers, and email addresses. Readers will find this list useful if they wish to locate the authors of specific pieces for feedback, comments, or questions. Further information is presented in a brief biographical sketch of each contributor that appears at the conclusion of each article. We publish this information to encourage "networking," which continues to be a valuable mainstay in the field of human resource development.

We are pleased with the high quality of material that is submitted for publication each year and often regret that we have page limitations. In addition, just as we cannot publish every manuscript we receive, you may find that not all published works are equally useful to you. Therefore, we encourage and invite ideas, materials, and suggestions that will help us to make subsequent *Annuals* as useful as possible to all of our readers.

Introduction
to the Experiential Learning Activities Section

Experiential learning activities ensure that lasting learning occurs. They should be selected with a specific learning objective in mind. These objectives are based on the participants' needs and the facilitator's skills. Although the experiential learning activities presented here vary in goals, group size, time required, and process, they all incorporate one important element: questions that ensure learning has occurred. This discussion, led by the facilitator, assists participants to process the activity, to internalize the learning, and to relate it to their day-to-day situations. It is this element that creates the unique experience and learning opportunity that only an experiential learning activity can bring to the group process.

Readers have used the *Annuals'* experiential learning activities for years to enhance their training and consulting events. Each learning experience is complete and includes all lecturettes, handout content, and other written material necessary to facilitate the activity. In addition, many include variations of the design that the facilitator might find useful. If the activity does not fit perfectly with your objectives, within your time frame, or to your group size, we encourage you to adapt the activity by adding your own variations. You will find additional experiential learning activities listed in the "Experiential Learning Activities Categories" chart that immediately follows this introduction.

The 2004 Pfeiffer Annual: Consulting includes twelve activities, in the following categories:

Individual Development: Sensory Awareness

Z Fantasy: Learning How to Haiku, by Edwina Pio

Individual Development: Diversity

Diversity from Within: Developing Leadership Sensitivity, by Steve Kuper

Individual Development: Life/Career Planning

Career Choice: Building Self-Knowledge, by Julia Panke Makela,
Pu-Shih Daniel Chen, and John A. Sample

Communication: Awareness

Taboo, Do I Know You? Introducing New People, by Joelle Davis Carter

Problem Solving: Generating Alternatives

Odyssey: Thinking Creatively, by Kristin J. Arnold

Groups: Negotiating/Bargaining

Why Don't You Want What I Want? Assessing Your Ability to Influence Others,
by Rick Maurer

Teams: How Groups Work

The Merry-Go-Round Project: Focusing on Leadership Style,
by Deborah Spring Laurel

Consulting and Facilitating: Facilitating: Skills

Search and Find: Discovering Expertise and Sharing Information,
by Cher Holton

Leadership: Styles

Hubris: Eliminating the Personal Delusion of Arrogance, by H.B. Karp

Mentor: Defining the Role, by Betsy Kendall and Mardy Wheeler

Organizations: Communication

Think Up the Organization: Building Awareness of Top-Management Concerns,
by W. Norman Gustafson

Organizations: Vision, Mission, Values, Strategy

"Those Who Matter": Group-Based Shareholder Analysis, by A. Venkat Raman

Locate other activities in these and other categories in the "Experiential Learning Activities Categories" chart that follows or in the comprehensive *Reference Guide to Handbooks and Annuals*. This guide, which is updated regularly, indexes all of the *Annuals* and all of the *Handbooks of Structured Experiences* that we have published to date. With each revision, the *Reference Guide* becomes a complete, up-to-date, and easy-to-use resource for selecting appropriate materials from all of the *Annuals* and *Hand-*

books. A print version of the *Reference Guide* is available for volumes through 1999. An online supplement covering the years through 2003 can be found at www.pfeiffer.com/go/supplement.

To further assist you in selecting appropriate ELAs, we provide the following grid that summarizes category, length of time, group size, and risk factor for each.

Category	ELA Title	Page	Time Required	Group Size	Risk Factor
Individual Development: Sensory Awareness	Z Fantasy	11	2 hours	6 to 30	Low
Individual Development: Diversity	Diversity from Within	23	45 to 60 minutes	15 to 30	Moderate
Individual Development: Life/Career Planning	Career Choice	27	60 to 70 minutes	15 to 30	Moderate
Communication: Awareness	Taboo, Do I Know You?	35	35 minutes before event; 55 minutes after event	10 to 60	Moderate
Problem Solving: Generating Alternatives	Odyssey	41	20 to 30 minutes	15 to 25	Low to Moderate
Groups: Negotiating/ Bargaining	Why Don't You Want What I Want?	45	45 minutes	10 to 30	Low to Moderate
Teams: How Groups Work	The Merry-Go-Round Project	51	Approximately 90 minutes	14 to 35	Moderate
Consulting and Facilitating: Facilitating Skills	Search and Find	63	1 to 3 hours	20 to 150	Moderate
Leadership: Styles	Hubris	69	Approximately 2.5 hours	Up to 24	Moderate to High
Leadership: Styles	Mentor	83	60 to 80 minutes	10 to 20	Moderate
Organizations: Communication	Think Up the Organization	91	90 minutes	20 to 30	Low
Organizations: Vision, Mission, Values, Strategy	"Those Who Matter"	97	2 to 3 hours	15 to 24	Moderate to High

Experiential Learning Activities Categories

Z Fantasy:
Learning How to Haiku

Activity Summary

This creative/spiritual activity uses haiku writing as a way to tap into the participants' personal awareness of their day-to-day experiences.

Goals

- To practice awareness as a step toward blending management and spirituality.

- To provide an atmosphere to compose haiku, weaving intuition and logic together.

Group Size

6 to 30 participants.

Time Required

Approximately 2 hours.

Materials

- A copy of the Z Fantasy Lecturette for the facilitator.

- Copies of the Z Fantasy How to Haiku worksheet for each participant.

- Copies of the Z Fantasy Suggested Readings for each participant.

- Blank paper for each participant.

- Pens or pencils for participants.

- Flip chart easel with paper/newsprint.

- Colored felt-tipped markers.

- Masking tape.

Physical Setting

A room large enough to accommodate the group size, for individual as well as small group work, with small tables and chairs. Alternatively carpets and floor cushions may be used. Outdoors or a garden is an enriching option.

Facilitating Risk Rating

Low.

Process

1. Announce the goals of the activity. *(1 minute.)*

2. Open with the following story on the need to weave spirituality and management into an acceptable framework for organizations:

   "The businessman rushed to the Zen master to get some techniques for giving his organization a competitive edge. He found the master amidst the flowers in the garden. Breathless to complete his task, for he had another urgent financial meeting to attend with his shareholders, he took a deep breath, and said: 'I understand that you have techniques for helping organizations reach their competitive advantage. Can you share some with me?' Unhurriedly, she invited him onto the porch and asked him to wait. After a few moments she emerged with an earthen teapot and a cup, which she set on the tiny table near him. She poured the steaming brew into the cup and went on pouring until it was overflowing. He could contain himself no longer, and exclaimed: 'Lady, what are you doing? The tea is spilling over! Let's just get on with the techniques.' She looked at him, and her eyes were piercingly gentle, as she said: 'You are like the cup, already full. How can anything be put in, unless you empty yourself?'"

   (5 minutes.)

3. Explain the concept by giving the Z Fantasy Lecturette and answering any questions.
   (10 minutes.)

4. Ask participants to sit comfortably with hands empty, eyes closed, and spine erect, as you lead them through an awareness exercise.

5. Use the following set of instructions, repeating them in a soft and soothing voice, with longer pauses between each repetition to give participants time to enter into their quietitude:

    > "Concentrate on your breathing. . . . Be aware of the air as it enters into your body and slowly moves out as you inhale deeply and exhale gently. . . . Relax your body. . . . Relax your mind. Do not cling to your thoughts, but let them move away like clouds wafting away in a summer breeze. . . . Continue to relax. . . . Feel your body loosening up. . . . Let the tensions from your neck and shoulders slowly and softly move out as you continue to breathe in and out. . . . Let your eyes relax, and your mouth and lips remain soft, as though you were about to smile. . . . Continue to breathe in and out slowly. . . . Relax and be rested. . . . Smile. . . . Continue to be aware of your breathing. . . ."

    You may repeat the instructions if you wish.
    (10 to 15 minutes.)

6. At the end of 10 to 12 minutes, depending on how much time you feel the group needs to relax, say: "After the next exhalation, slowly come back to this place and slowly open your eyes. . . . Wait for a few moments in silence."

7. Ask participants to share how they feel right now. Invite them to talk about the experience and what happened to their awareness.
    (5 to 10 minutes.)

8. Distribute the Z Fantasy How to Haiku worksheet and pens or pencils. Tell participants to work individually, in silence, to complete it. Participants may wish to move around, or sit in silence as they haiku. Move among the participants and be available for clarification during this time.
    (20 minutes.)

9. Ask participants to share their haiku. Encourage participants who share with applause and verbal reinforcement, emphasizing that we must honor the muse in each person.
    (10 minutes.)

10. Now ask participants to get in touch with the reason why they chose to write the particular haiku they did and the insights they may have had in the process. Give them some silent time.
    (5 minutes.)

11. Divide the participants into small groups. Ask them to share their haiku and insights in these groups. If participants wish to put up their haiku, make available the flip chart paper, marker pens, and masking tape.
    (20 minutes.)

12. After all participants have had a chance to share within the small groups, re-convene the participants, and ask each group for common themes. Summa-rize major points from the entire group and post them on the flip chart. *(15 minutes.)*

13. Debrief the experience by leading a discussion around the following questions:

    - How could you do this type of activity on a regular basis?

    - What are your plans to continue to enrich your life?

    - How feasible is your plan?

    - What barriers exist to your plan?

    - Who else can you share this technique with?
    (15 to 20 minutes.)

14. End with the following story:

    "And so it was that a tired business executive, while traveling to one more marketing meeting, saw a man who had a deep whimsical smile. Curious, she watched him as they sat in the departure lounge. He came and sat by her and gently said, 'I would like to tell you a story about a person just like you.' Surprised, she nodded in assent.

    "The Zen master spoke about a beautiful stream that moved through the forests and glades and was very successful in its movement. But one day, after many years, it flowed to the edge of a desert. Hesitantly, it tried to cross, but was swallowed up by the sand. It thought of how it had moved earlier and called to mind its past experiences, then tried once more, with determina-tion and strategy, to cross, but again failed. In utter frustration, the stream stood still.

    "And as it stood still, it heard the wind whisper, 'Let me take you up in my arms and put you down on the other side.' 'What?' asked the stream in amaze-ment. 'To do that I would have to totally change my behavior and known pat-terns, and evaporate so you can carry me across, and I may lose myself in the process.' 'There is no other way,' the stream heard the wind say, 'if you want to cross the desert.' So the stream gave itself up into the wind and was wafted along, until it fell as rain on the other side of the desert and resumed its orig-inal essence.

    "Quietly the Zen master said, 'Perhaps you need to be like the stream,' as the departure call was announced."

15. Silently hand out copies of the Z Fantasy Suggested Readings and close the workshop.

Variations

- This activity can be done across organizations, within one organization, or for management students.

- If the group size is small, each participant can be asked to compose two or three haiku in Step 8.

- After Step 10, participants can be encouraged to compose one more haiku on the same theme or to redraft their current one.

- If participants are from the same organization, the group may be asked to work on emergent themes.

- The entire group can compose one haiku for the end of the activity.

Submitted by Edwina Pio.

Edwina Pio, Ph.D., *blends the intricacies of management, psychology, and spirituality in her teaching, writing, and consultancy. Her work takes her to Europe, India, the United States, and New Zealand, where she enjoys leading people to the threshold of their minds. She is passionate about yoga and meditation and incorporates them in her work. Currently she lives in New Zealand, where she teaches management at the Auckland University of Technology and works with women and children who are experiencing domestic violence.*

Z Fantasy Lecturette

Z fantasy is the realm of divergent thinking, creativity, the weaving of intuition and logic. Organizations in this century must be able to come up with products, processes, and services that are niche, aesthetic, and earth-nourishing. No longer can humankind take from the treasures of the earth without giving back in stewardship of the universe, both for today's and for future generations. In the same vein, management must seek for ways to address the yearning of the human spirit for a more harmonious world. In the last few years, organizations have been actively searching for methodologies, procedures, and policies to blend spirit and management in an attempt to garner the commitment, competence, and creativity of their people.

Spirit is used here, not as in wearing a particular religious garb, but in the sense of energy, life force, breath of life (prana in Sanskrit, chi in Chinese, pneuma in Greek, spiritus in Latin). Hence, spirituality is tapping into this life force so that the individual and organization, in their reciprocal influence on each other, thrive in the business world and in the personal world.

Z fantasy seeks to ignite and rekindle individuals in the organization. A necessary prerequisite for this is awareness, or dhayana in Sanskrit, jhana in Pali, chan in Chinese, and Zen in Japanese. This meditative stance leads to the composition of haiku.

Haiku is a form of Japanese poetry, containing seventeen syllables, in three phrases of five-seven-five syllables, or just three short lines, although its modern form ranges from fifteen to twenty-five syllables. It usually presents a crystalline moment of heightened awareness in simple imagery, traditionally using an image from nature. It is a way of calling the spirit of the thing named, with the eternal and momentary juxtaposed. It is considered poetry of ahness, because it makes you say, "Aha, now I see it!" The last line is generally given a twist, a bit of satire and punch! It is also an awareness practice with healing power.

Among the famous Zen poets are Issa, Bahso, Buson, and Chiyo-ni. Some examples of their work are available in bookstores or online.

Haiku focuses on brevity, capturing the essence of the situation, and literally forcing organizational team members to get to the core of the problem, creating an Archimedean "eureka!" for themselves, and maybe for the organization as well. Some more recent haiku compositions with current themes are

> Saying goodbye to layoffs
> Learning continuously . . .
> Not autumn, but spring.

Lands of burning oil
Extraction, fueling time.
Freedom sold for pennies.

Would that I could learn. . .
From hairy caterpillar
To colored butterfly.

Vision, mission, wow!
Goals, objectives, strategic planning.
But where is my soul?

Triple bottom line,
Earth nourishing, wonderful . . .
Spread like a virus.

Z fantasy is at the heart of our travels into spirituality at work. It addresses the need for organizations to stay alive and buoyant, to be passionate and profitable, with a sense of fun and laughter, to focus on the essence of the issue, and to have the ability to continuously create new ways of doing and being.

The Zen master would say: "Life is measured not by the moments we breathe, but the moments that take our breath away!"

Z Fantasy How to Haiku

Instructions: Please complete the checklist below by placing a tick mark in the boxes that apply to you. You may add in your own elements in the blank boxes.

In this organization, my spirit feels:

☐ Harmonious

☐ Fragmented

☐ Tired

☐ Excited

☐ Peaceful

☐ Challenged

☐ Routinized

☐ Depressed

☐ _____

☐ _____

☐ _____

☐ _____

☐ _____

How would you like your spirit to feel within an organization? Write a few sentences about this in the space provided below:

Haiku happenings:

- Poetry of seventeen syllables

- Three lines of five-seven-five syllables

- Essence of the situation is portrayed

- Images from nature are used

- Transitory nature of life is presented

- Playfulness and humor are incorporated

- Both logic and intuition are ingredients

Now call to mind one issue or concern that you are dealing with in your life, and select the key theme. Keeping this theme as the focus, pick up one or two related elements, people, policies, strategies, products, or processes emanating from it. Please put these thoughts into your haiku draft below. Enjoy! Feel the freedom of serious play!

Draft 1

Draft 2

Draft 3

Version 1.0

Version 1.1

Remember, your haiku may be composed in the first draft. If you are getting stuck, unstick yourself. Take a few deep breaths. Go for a silent walk.

Z Fantasy Suggested Readings

Ashmos, D.P., & Duchon, D. (2000). Spirituality at work: A conceptualisation and measure. *Journal of Management Inquiry, 9(2)*, 134–145.

Donegan, P., & Ishibashi, Y. (1998). *Chiyo-ni: Woman haiku master.* Tokyo: Tuttle Publishing.

Gunther, M. (2001). God business. *Fortune, 144(1)*, 59–80.

Hamill, S. (trns.) (1997). *The spring of my life.* Boston, MA: Shambhala.

Handy, C. (2002). What's a business for? *Harvard Business Review, 80(12)*.

Higinson, W.J. (1996). *The haiku seasons.* Tokyo: Kodansha International.

Kaican, J. (Ed.). (1996). *Snow on the water.* Winchester, VA: Red Moon Press.

King, R.H. (2001). *Thomas Merton and Thich Nhat Hanh: Engaged spirituality in an age of globalisation.* New York: Continuum International Publishing.

Kodama, M., & Yanagishima, H. (1999). *The Zen fool Ryokan.* Boston, MA: Charles E. Tuttle Co.

Pio, E. (2003). *Z biz-The art of wealth: Stepping stones for spirituality in organizations.* Working paper.

Warriner, W. (1991). *Corporate haiku.* London: HarperCollins.

Diversity from Within:
Developing Leadership Sensitivity

Activity Summary

A brief activity that allows leaders to safely explore how their experiences have influenced their leadership styles.

Goals

- To help participants share their own backgrounds and personal ideals with others.

- To determine how one's background influences leadership style.

- To use this information to develop a sensitivity to diversity in one's workplace.

Group Size

15 to 30 participants of diverse backgrounds. All participants should be managers/leaders within the same organization.

Time Required

45 to 60 minutes.

Materials

- A sheet of newsprint and a marker for each participant.

- A flip chart and felt-tipped markers.

- Masking tape.

Physical Setting

A room with round tables and chairs.

Facilitating Risk Rating

Moderate.

Preparation

Before the activity begins, post sheets of flip-chart paper on the walls—one page for each participant. Also prepare one flip-chart page with the following questions:

- What's your name?

- Where do you call home?

- What's the warmest room (emotionally) in your house? Why do you say this? What makes it different?

- What has been handed down to you ethnically (for example, food, values, holidays) that has caused you to appreciate your ethnic heritage the most?

Place the easel where the questions can be seen easily.

Process

1. Open the activity by defining diversity as: "the state or fact of being diverse; difference; variety; multiformity; a point of difference."

2. Tell participants that openness about oneself and appreciation for others will be explored during this activity.

3. Have each participant take a marker to one of the posted newsprint pages and write their answers to the questions that you have posted on the easel. *(10 minutes.)*

4. Open a large group discussion with participants' responses to the questions. Ask what similarities and differences they see in their responses, especially to the last question. Post responses on the flip chart. *(15 minutes.)*

5. Once everyone has had a chance to contribute, ask participants to form trios and discuss how they think their personal backgrounds have affected their leadership styles. Remind them to trade off so that everyone has time to contribute. *(10 minutes.)*

6. Ask each group to report out, posting the results. Conclude by leading a discussion based on the following questions:

   - What have you learned about yourself from your discussion with others in your group?

   - What have you learned about the diversity of others in your group?

   - What qualities would you like to develop within yourself to become more sensitive to others' differences from you?

   - How have others' differences affected their leadership styles in a positive way?

   - How can you translate what you've learned to your own role as a leader?

   (10 to 15 minutes.)

—————

Submitted by Steve Kuper.

Steve Kuper, *principal and founder of Innovative Learning Strategies, LLC, has over twenty years of experience and expertise in training, designing, and facilitating training programs at places such as United Airlines, Kimberly-Clark Corporation, and the College of Southern Maryland. The Innovative Learning philosophy of "working within to bring out the best" is a simple idea that brings great impact. The team at Innovative Learning is committed to the concept of a fun, interactive environment where the seminar participants work to bring change to both their personal and professional lives.*

Career Choice:
Building Self-Knowledge

Activity Summary

This activity stimulates exploration and discussion of the integral role that values play, both in personal career development and in the culture of various work environments.

Goals

- To provide an opportunity for participants to contemplate their own values.

- To increase participants' knowledge regarding the role that values have played in their career choices.

- To introduce the concept of work environments supporting employee values and start participants thinking about possible career changes.

Group Size

15 to 30 participants who are interested in changing or enhancing their careers.

Time Required

60 to 70 minutes.

Materials

- Career Choice Lecturette for the facilitator.

- Copies of the Career Choice Model for all participants.

- (Optional) Overhead projector and a transparency of the model.

- Three to six 3" x 5" cards on which are written off-the-wall values suggestions, such as Legos®, crayons, my teddy bear, puppies, coffee, or bell bottom pants.

- Blank 3" x 5" note cards or paper squares, three per participant.

- Pens or pencils for participants.

- Small basket, bag, or hat.

- Flip chart and markers.

Physical Setting

A room large enough to allow participants to walk around and to interact with one another.

Facilitating Risk Rating

Moderate.

Trainer Note

Discussion of personal values can be a challenging or discomforting topic for some individuals. To minimize these concerns, consider the presentation environment, be sensitive to participants' concerns, and allow for the use of individual discretion in sharing personal information.

Process

1. Begin by discussing self-knowledge and values as they pertain to one's choice of career. Say:

    "Today, we will focus on a very important foundation piece for career development—knowing about ourselves. In particular we will be talking about our values—about what is desirable or important to us—and how those values relate to both our personal choices about a career and about our sense of belonging in our work environments. We will get a glimpse of why values are critical for our careers and professional development."

    (5 minutes.)

2. Say that they will be given an opportunity to consider how their own values have played a role in their choice of careers and whether or not their work environments support these values. Answer any questions and then move on to the Career Choice Lecturette. Hand out copies of the Career Choice

Model (or display it on an overhead projector) to allow people to follow along as you talk.
(10 minutes.)

3. After finishing the lecturette, answer any questions that people may have.
    (10 minutes.)

4. Give three 3" x 5" note cards and a pen or pencil to each participant. Ask them to write one of their most important values on each card. Tell participants that the more imaginative and unusual the suggestion, the better.
    (5 minutes.)

5. Ask participants to fold each completed note card in half and place them in the basket [bag, hat]. After you have collected all of them, *add the prepared cards*, shake the bag to mix the cards up, and ask participants to draw three cards that are not their own from the bag.

6. Then give them 10 minutes to "scamper"—stand up, move about the room, and trade cards with others. The goal is for each person to acquire a final set of three values that he or she feels are a good match. Encourage participation from those who are less involved.
    (10 minutes.)

7. Call time and guide a discussion of the activity using the following questions:

    • Did you find it easy or difficult to choose three values to write on the cards?

    • How did you choose the three values? Where did you learn them?

    • When you initially received your "new values" from the basket, what was your reaction? Did you receive values that you also hold? Did you receive any that did not fit your value system?

    • How did you feel about your "new values"? Do you prefer the new values or your original values?

    • In swapping the value cards, did you find any that surprised you? How about any that you did not originally think of but that you hold?

    • What values were "hot commodities" for trading?

    • What values did you have a hard time swapping, that is, getting rid of?

    • What type of work environment may fit the final set of values you hold? Would you foresee any conflicts with working in this type of environment?

- If you found yourself in a work environment that supported values that conflicted with yours, how would you address this?

- Would you most likely integrate the environment's values or would you resist them? Would you stay in that work environment?

- What factors would influence your decision to stay or to leave?

- How could you explore what values may be supported prior to joining an organization?

- What kind of decision-making style do you have and does it need to be adjusted as you seek a career change?

- What do you think was most significant about this experience?

- What will you do differently now in respect to your career, either returning to your present workplace or seeking a new job?
  (30 minutes.)

Variation

- With groups larger than 30, use two or more baskets to speed up the collection and distribution process, making sure that each basket holds some of your own "off-the-wall" suggestions. Then divide the participants into a few small groups to discuss the questions and report out to the large group. Note that larger groups will require more time.

Submitted by Julia Panke Makela, Pu-Shih Daniel Chen, and John A. Sample.

Julia Panke Makela, M.S., Ed.S., *is a program specialist at The Graduate School, USDA's Center for Leadership and Management, where she coordinates and co-facilitates all aspects of the Senior Executive Service Developmental Seminars and the Congressional Fellows Program. She holds graduate degrees in both counseling and education from Florida State University and is a nationally certified counselor, specializing in career development.*

Pu-Shih Daniel Chen, M.S., *is a doctoral student in educational leadership and policy studies at the Florida State University. His research interests include moral and spiritual development, assessment of educational outcomes, and using technology in higher education.*

John A. Sample, Ph.D., SPHR, *is a visiting assistant professor in the adult education and human resource development program, College of Education, Florida State University. He teaches graduate courses in adult learning, human resources, and organizational development.*

Career Choice Lecturette

Four things are critical to consider when making a career choice:

1. Being clear about what you want (your personal values).

2. Knowing your options.

3. Knowing your decision-making style.

4. Understanding how your innermost thoughts influence your decision making.

Look at the Career Choice Model handout and note the relationship among these. The foundation of an effective career choice is laid by developing our knowledge of self, particularly our values, and knowing what career options allow us to remain true to them. Next, having a decision-making strategy allows us to make effective choices based on what we know about ourselves and the choices we have career-wise. Finally, throughout the entire process, the decisions we make are influenced by our innermost thoughts and feelings. Negative thoughts (such as self-doubt) constrain us from making effective career choices, while positive thoughts (such as confidence in our abilities) help facilitate our making effective career choices.

We must know the following about ourselves:

- Our Values—What do we think is important or desirable?

- Our Interests—What do we enjoy doing?

- Our Skills—What abilities do we have?

Values are an especially important consideration for each of us because researchers have demonstrated that people who live according to their values show greater levels of job satisfaction and self-esteem than those who do not (Reardon, Lenz, Sampson, & Peterson, 2000). To take this one step further, our self-esteem has been shown to be positively related to our job performance, organizational citizenship behavior, and organizational commitment (Kreitner & Kinicki, 1998).

In choosing a career or making a career change, you must address questions such as:

- What types of opportunities are available to me?

- Where might I go to pursue these opportunities?

- What resources can help me get there?

Once we have answers to these questions, we can move up to the next level of the pyramid, knowing how we make decisions and adjusting our behavior accordingly. There are many different ways to make decisions. Some of us want to talk through everything with others before coming to a conclusion, while others think things through quietly before saying a word. Some want to make specific lists and follow preset procedures, while others rely on gut feelings. All of these methods are effective and serve different purposes. For instance, a decision maker who likes to research and plan out every step may find this strategy particularly helpful when buying a house. Yet this person may drive friends crazy by applying the same strategy to picking a restaurant. The key is to understand your preferred style and to match it to the style called for by the decision at hand. Making a career choice may require you to use a more thoughtful, analytical style than you usually use, or you may be stuck and unable to make a decision because you are too intent on analyzing every nuance of a career choice.

The final factor in making a career choice concerns your underlying thinking. As you can probably imagine, negative thoughts about oneself hinder one's ability to make and act on career decisions (for example, "I never make good decisions" or "I always sound foolish when I call to ask if there are any openings"). On the other hand, positive thoughts help one to move forward ("I make the best decisions that I can with the information that I have" or "I know that I am a capable and qualified candidate for this position"). The ability to have positive thoughts affects every level of the pyramid and can be the most critical for making career choices.

References

Kreitner, R., & Kinicki, A. (1998). *Organizational behavior* (4th ed.). New York: Irwin/ McGraw-Hill.

Peterson, G.W., Sampson, J.P., Jr., Reardon, R.C., & Lenz, J.G. (in press). A cognitive information processing approach to career problem solving and decision making. In D. Brown (Ed.), *Career choice and development*. San Francisco, CA: Jossey-Bass.

Reardon, R.C., Lenz, J.G., Sampson, J.P., & Peterson, G.W. (2000). *Career development and planning: A comprehensive approach*. Belmont, CA: Brooks/Cole.

Sampson, J.P., Jr., Peterson, G.W., Lenz, J.G., & Reardon, R.C. (1992). A cognitive approach to career services: Translating concepts into practice. *The Career Development Quarterly, 41*(1), 67–74.

Career Choice Model

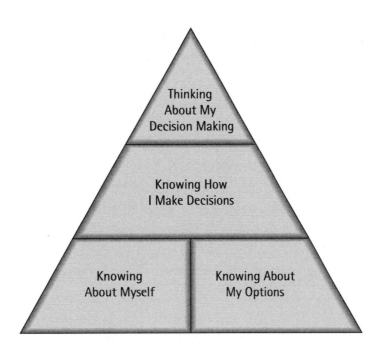

Adapted from J.P. Sampson, Jr., G.W. Peterson, J.G. Lenz, & R.C. Reardon. (1992). A cognitive approach to career services: Translating concepts into practice. *The Career Development Quarterly, 41*(1), 67–74. Used with permission.

Taboo, Do I Know You?
Introducing New People

Activity Summary

An interactive small group activity that allows participants who do not know one another to introduce themselves at the beginning of a workshop and then process the experience at the end.

Goals

- To encourage participants to critically process how they view themselves and others based on initial interactions.

- To create a safe environment for participants to reflect on themselves and share with other participants.

- To establish a foundation for teamwork and group collaboration.

Group Size

12 to 60 participants in a training session of some sort, divided into small groups of 6 to 8.

Time Required

35 minutes at the beginning and 55 minutes near the end of an event.

Materials

- One Taboo Round I sheet for each person.

- One Taboo Round II sheet for each person.

- Pens or pencils for each participant.

Physical Setting

A room large enough to accommodate up to 10 groups of 6 to 8 individuals.

Facilitating Risk Rating

Moderate.

Trainer Note

This activity is most effective when groups are kept small and intimate and when people truly do not know one another well. It serves as preparation for more complex large and small group activities to follow. Due to the personal nature of the exercise, it is important that you encourage participants to be honest about their feelings and elaborate on their statements. In certain settings, participants can be reserved and reluctant to talk about themselves, so you have to be creative to ensure that everyone contributes and is involved. Additionally, be prepared to develop additional process questions based on the nature of the small groups.

Process

1. Introduce the goals and purpose of the activity by saying: "This activity will allow us to get to know each other better and gain an in-depth understanding of all group members. It is important that everyone actively participate and engage so that the desired goals are met."

2. Disseminate the Taboo Round I sheets and pens or pencils. Ask participants to break into groups of 6 or 8 and to select a facilitator for each group who is willing to assist in keeping the process moving.

3. Ask participants to write their names on the top line of the Taboo Round I sheets. Once all participants have written their names, say, "At this point, pass your sheets to your left. When you receive the sheet passed to you, look at the name at the top and write one word or short phrase that you think describes that person, based on the *initial interactions* you have had with each other thus far. Take no more than 20 seconds to write on each sheet. Continue passing the sheets to your left until your original sheet is returned to you." Survey the group to ensure everyone has finished.
    (5 minutes.)

4. Ask whether all participants have their own sheets. Ask for a volunteer to begin the introductions by first stating his or her name and reading the words or phrases that group members have written on his or her sheet. Then ask the in-

dividual to add descriptors and characteristics that *are not* listed on the sheet. You may wish to provide an example: "My name is . . . and the following words and phrases are listed (1) smart, (2) courteous, and (3) nice smile. I would add hard working and loyal to those."

5. After gaining consensus that everyone understands, ask for volunteers until each participant has been introduced.

   (10 to 20 minutes, depending on the number of participants.)

6. Once the introductions are complete, ask the following questions:

   - What did you learn about each other beyond initial contact and interaction? Did you learn more or less than you assumed about these other people?

   - Was the activity difficult for you? In what way? Why do you think that was true?

   Allow about 5 or 6 minutes for participants to volunteer and provide feedback on these questions and additional ones that may be relevant to your group.

   (10 minutes.)

7. Reiterate the goals of the activity and, based on the nature of the event (full day training, workshop, seminar, or retreat), say, "During the course of this [retreat, seminar], you will be working closely with each other and I encourage you to collaborate as a team. One of the most important aspects of collaborative learning is being able to know people beneath the surface. We will repeat this activity prior to the end of this program."

8. Collect all the Taboo Round I sheets from the participants. (You will return them to participants after Round II at the conclusion of the program.)

9. As the workshop or session draws to a close, bring the small group participants back together for Round II. Distribute the Taboo Round II sheet and repeat steps 3 through 5 of this activity.

   (15 to 20 minutes.)

10. After the process is complete, ask the group the following questions:

    - Was the activity harder or easier in this round? Why was that?

    - What was different from the first round?

    - Describe some of the things that have occurred during this program that may have contributed to your having the same or different perspectives of other group members at this time.

    (10 minutes.)

11. After the discussion, redistribute the Taboo Round I sheets and ask the group members to compare what is written on the two sheets.

12. After providing about 3 minutes for review, summarize the process and lead a discussion with these questions:

- What are the pros and cons of assumptions and first impressions?

- Did the first round of the activity impact your interaction with another group member? In what way?

- If I were to say the old adage, "Don't judge a book by its cover," what would you reply after this activity? In what ways, if any, did this experience provide you with different insights about knowing and understanding other people?

- What would you do differently in terms of meeting and getting to know people as a result of what you have learned?

  (10 minutes.)

Submitted by Joelle Davis Carter.

Joelle Davis Carter *is the founder and chief operating officer of RJC Consulting, LLC. The company specializes in providing customized training programs and seminars, coaching and skill enhancement tools, assessment and program evaluation, facilitation and consultation services, and training curriculum development. She has prepared and presented over thirty programs on leadership assessment and development, diversity and sensitivity issues, and organization development. Clients include higher education institutions, nonprofit organizations, corporations, and community-based agencies.*

Taboo Round I

Your name: _____

_____

_____

_____

_____

_____

_____

_____

_____

_____

_____

_____

_____

_____

Taboo Round II

Your name: _____

_____

_____

_____

_____

_____

_____

_____

_____

_____

_____

_____

_____

Odyssey:
Thinking Creatively

Activity Summary

A brief activity that encourages creative problem solving and energizes a group.

Goal

- To encourage participants to think unconventionally and creatively.

Group Size

15 to 25 people.

Time Required

20 to 30 minutes, depending on group size.

Materials

- 4 to 5 interesting household objects that could conceivably be used for several purposes, such as an extension cord, unique cooking utensil, office item, or a tool.

Physical Setting

A space large enough for all participants to see one another.

Facilitating Risk Rating

Low to moderate.

Process

1. Introduce this activity as a way to challenge our creativity, think unconventionally, and be creative.

2. Ask whether anyone is aware of the Odyssey of the Mind program from Creative Competitions, Inc. If no one volunteers, share the origins and purpose of the program:

   "Sponsored by NASA, among others, Odyssey of the Mind is a school program designed to foster creative thinking and problem-solving skills among students from kindergarten through college. Students solve problems in a variety of areas with a variety of different tools. By encouraging children to solve problems in a creative and unique way as a team, the program helps them to learn lifelong skills, such as working as a team, evaluating ideas, making decisions, and creating solutions, while developing self-confidence from their experiences."

3. Now that the participants know what Odyssey of the Mind is all about, encourage them to think differently about the first object you have in your hand. For example, take an extension cord and wrap it up, then display it where everyone can see. Say that it could be an extension cord (traditional thinking) or it could be a whip. Or it could be a lasso. Ask for other creative ideas. *(3 minutes.)*

4. Tell the group that you are going to pass "something" around the room, and as each person receives it he or she is to explain to the rest of the participants what it could be. (Tell them that it is okay to pass if they don't have an idea to share quickly. Otherwise, you can get bogged down.)

5. Hand one of the other objects to one of the participants and ask him or her to think creatively. Ask, "What could this be?" *(3 minutes.)*

6. Pass the item among all participants and then introduce one or two other objects. *(5 minutes.)*

7. Use the following questions to debrief and summarize this activity:

   - What inspired your creativity?

   - What made it difficult to be creative?

   - Did you become more or less creative as you listened to others' ideas?

- How can you apply this lesson when your work group is required to be creative?

- How can you transfer what you learned into working with thoughts and ideas, rather than physical objects?

(10 minutes.)

Submitted by Kristin J. Arnold.

Kristin J. Arnold, M.B.A. C.P.C.M., *specializes in coaching executives and their leadership, management, and employee teams, particularly in the areas of strategic and business planning, process improvement, decision making, and collaborative problem solving. An accomplished author and editor of several professional articles and books, as well as a featured columnist in* The Daily Press, *a Tribune Publishing newspaper, she is regarded as an expert in team development and process improvement techniques. She has provided process facilitation, training, and coaching support to both public and private sector initiatives.*

Why Don't You Want What I Want?
Assessing Your Ability to Influence Others

Activity Summary

A quick and easy activity useful for pinpointing specific ways to increase support for and reduce resistance to one's ideas.

Goals

- To identify characteristics that increase others' support of one's ideas.

- To assess the level to which participants utilize these means in specific instances when requiring support.

Group Size

10 to 30 participants.

Time Required

45 minutes.

Materials

- One copy of the Why Don't You Want What I Want? Assessment for each participant.

- Pencils or pens for participants.

- Flip chart and markers.

Physical Setting

A table and chairs for participants.

Facilitating Risk Rating

Low to moderate, depending on the depth of discussion.

Process

1. Ask how many participants have ever asked themselves, "Why don't they want what I want?" or "Why can't she see it my way?" or "Why is he fighting me about this good idea?" After a show of hands, say that we have all wondered why it is so difficult to sell a good idea to others.

2. Ask participants what they have done in the past when they were successful in selling an idea to someone else. Note their suggestions on a flip-chart page.

3. Say to participants:

    "When we attempt to influence others or interest them and gain their commitment to our ideas, we need support at three levels. First, in *understanding* our idea. Does the person "*get*" it? Second, we need a *positive reaction* to our idea. Does the person *like* it? Third, we need a *positive relationship* with the person. Does the person *trust* us and have confidence in us? It is in our own best interest to encourage support and minimize resistance at all three levels.

    "Although it may be challenging to increase support and minimize resistance, there are six principles that increase our chances of being successful. We're going to learn about them now."

    (10 minutes.)

4. Provide copies of the Why Don't You Want What I Want? Assessment and pens or pencils for all participants and ask them to complete it. Tell them that they may find it easier to consider a single person or situation as they fill out the Assessment. Explain that it is human nature to react differently in different situations or to be dependent on the relationships we have with different individuals. Reassure them that they will not need to share any of their responses or scores with anyone.

    (15 minutes.)

5. Once everyone has completed the Assessment and scored it, ask what was most difficult for them about completing it. Note that their scores would most likely change if they considered different individuals and situations.

6. Say:

    "If you are interested in improving your scores in specific situations with specific individuals, begin by noticing how others implement the six characteristics when they gain support for their ideas. Select the *one* characteristic on which you are most interested in improving. Challenge yourself to shift how you approach and respond to others. Begin by selecting low-risk situations and new ways of approaching and responding to other people in order to influence them."

7. Remind them that mixed scores (some high, some low) suggest that they are most likely effective to some extent, but could be even more so. Suggest that participants complete the Assessment again at another time for a different situation with another person to determine whether low scores are because of the situation or the individual. (Give out additional copies of the Assessment, if desired.)

8. Debrief the activity by leading a discussion around these questions.

   - What did you learn about gaining support for your ideas?

   - What did you learn about yourself?

   - About the way you deal with other people?

   - Which of the six areas requires the most attention for you to be successful?

   - What will you do differently in the future when you want to influence someone else?

   - How will you transfer what you have learned about yourself today to your personal life? to your workplace?

   (10 minutes.)

Submitted by Rick Mauer.

Rick Maurer *assists individuals and organizations to build support for their ideas, such as major changes inside the organization. Based in Arlington, Virginia, he has worked with companies, government agencies, and non-profits in many countries since he founded Maurer & Associates in 1978. He is author of five books, including* Beyond the Wall of Resistance *(Bard, 1996),* Feedback Toolkit *(Productivity Press, 1994), and* Why Don't You Want What I Want? *(Bard, 2002).*

Why Don't You Want What I Want? Assessment

In *Why Don't You Want What I Want?* (2002), Rick Mauer suggests that support and resistance are two sides of a single coin. When we attempt to influence others—interest them and ask them to commit to our ideas—we need support at three levels. Level 1 focuses on understanding. Do people "get" it or don't they? Level 2 focuses on the emotional reaction people have to the idea itself. Do they like it or dislike it? And Level 3 focuses on our relationship with the other person or group. Does he or she have trust and confidence in us or not? When resistance is active at even one level, our chance of success diminishes. Obviously, it is in our own best interests to encourage support in all three areas and minimize resistance at any of the levels.

At times, knowing how to increase support and minimize resistance can be extremely challenging. Maurer's study of people who are consistently successful in getting their ideas across often demonstrates the six principles covered in the assessment below.

Instructions: Identify a challenging situation and consider a single person or a group as you complete the assessment. This is not a personality assessment; how you respond will be based on *the situation you are in.* Your scores would most likely change if you considered different individuals and groups.

Use a 7-point scale for each item. Circle the number that indicates where you are on a continuum with the two statements at either end. Be as candid as you can be.

1. I have a *clear intention* that embraces my needs and theirs.

Often my intention is to implement my idea without regard to what the other person wants.				My relationship with the other person is as important to me as the idea I am trying to get across is.		
1	2	3	4	5	6	7

2. I consider the *context.*

Often I present my ideas without regard for the context, such as the business environment, history of similar ideas, or the person's relationship with me.				I consider a wide range of contextual cues before presenting my ideas.		
1	2	3	4	5	6	7

3. I avoid *knee-jerk reactions.*

   I often react defensively if something triggers an emotional response.

   I know what triggers defense responses when I am engaged, and I have developed effective ways to avoid reacting without thinking.

   1   2   3   4   5   6   7

4. I *pay attention.*

   I focus entirely on stating my points clearly.

   I pay attention to subtle cues to let me know if I am on or off track.

   1   2   3   4   5   6   7

5. I explore *differences* deeply.

   When I work with this person, I avoid criticism and negative emotional reactions to my ideas.

   I encourage criticism and strong emotional reactions to my ideas.

   1   2   3   4   5   6   7

6. I find ways to *connect.*

   Others need to grow up. If I say someone should do something, he or she should just do it.

   I allow myself to be influenced by what I hear from others and seek ways to create a mutual win.

   1   2   3   4   5   6   7

Scoring and Interpretation

Scoring a 6 or a 7 on all items: Assuming you're not delusional, you are probably quite effective in interesting others in your ideas and gaining their commitment to implement them.

Scoring a 3 to 5 on all items: You may often ask yourself: Why don't they want what I want? Your success may be highly situational. There are probably times when you are very influential and others where you consistently fall short.

Scoring a 1 or 2 on all items: Give yourself a lot of credit for taking such a close look at your actions.

Mixed scores (some high, some low): Take a look at the low scores, these areas may lower your effectiveness on consulting engagements or in leadership situations. Begin the change process by noticing how people who seem to be effective at putting their ideas across handle those areas where you scored low. Note what they do. Then build on your strengths and begin to incorporate one or two new actions you have learned into what you are already doing well.

Start slowly. Changing how we view situations and other people and then changing our behavior doesn't come easily. Starting small can allow the snowball to get larger. Starting too big often leads to frustration.

Reference

Mauer, R. (2002). *Why don't you want what I want?* Austin, TX: Bard Press.

The Merry-Go-Round Project:
Focusing on Leadership Style

Activity Summary

A mildly physical activity that allows participants to experience and evaluate the impact of planning and buy-in on a project team's results.

Goals

- To provide a model for planning a team project.

- To develop the participants' awareness of the impact of different project leadership styles on project results.

- To test the effectiveness of project leadership behaviors in response to simulated real-job obstructions and challenges.

Group Size

14 to 35 participants from the same organization or department in table groups of 7 participants.

Time Required

Approximately 90 minutes.

Materials

- One Tinkertoy® Colossal construction sets (with 142 pieces) for each group of 7 participants.

- A Merry-Go-Round Project Background Information sheet for the facilitator.

- A Merry-Go-Round Project Planning sheet for each participant.

- A Merry-Go-Round Project Construction Instructions sheet for each project leader.

- A Merry-Go-Round Project Observer Briefing sheet for each observer.

- One or two Merry-Go-Round Project Voice of Reality Briefing sheets for each subgroup.

- A Merry-Go-Round Project Summary sheet for each participant.

- Pencils or pens for all participants.

Physical Setting

A room large enough for 2 to 5 round or rectangular tables that each seat 5 participants, with 5 chairs at each table. (*Note:* The 3 to 5 participants involved in the actual construction of the merry-go-round will be seated at the table. The 2 volunteers serving as the Voice of Reality and the Observer will be standing.)

Facilitating Risk Rating

Moderate.

Process

1. Organize the participants into project teams, with 5 to 7 participants at each table. Have them clear off the surface of the table so that they have plenty of space.

2. Place one Tinkertoy construction set on each table, with the instruction not to open the sets until given the go-ahead.

3. Introduce the Merry-Go-Round Project by reading through the Merry-Go-Round Project Background Information sheet.
   (5 minutes.)

4. Explain that only one person at each table will be the Project Leader. However, each participant should complete a Merry-Go-Round Project Planning sheet. Hand these sheets out at this point, along with pens or pencils.
   (10 minutes.)

5. Ask the group: "Why should everyone complete the Project Planning sheet, even though only one person at each table grouping will be the actual Project Leader?" Ensure that they recognize the fact that all team members come to a project with their own ideas regarding how to organize and implement

the project. Because of this, the Project Leader will need to obtain their buy-in to the Project Leader's vision and plan, which can be problematic.
(5 minutes.)

6. Appoint a Project Leader at each table, handing that person the Merry-Go-Round Construction Instructions. Tell the Project Leaders that it will be left to their discretion to decide whether to show the diagram and instructions to their teams.

7. Ask for two volunteers from each group and ask them to join you in the hall for a briefing. Tell the remaining participants that, during your absence, they may dump out the contents of their Tinkertoy containers and organize the contents. However, they are *not* to begin with any discussion of the project until the other players have returned.

8. In the hall, hand out the Merry-Go-Round Project Observer Briefing sheet and the Merry-Go-Round Project Voice of Reality Briefing sheets to the volunteers, one of each for each group.

9. Explain the role of the Voice of Reality and read through the briefing sheet. Emphasize the importance of making the project interruptions as realistic and as frequent as possible. Indicate that they should feel free to be as creative as they like. However, caution the volunteers that they should ensure that their project groups are actually able to complete construction of their Merry-Go-Rounds within the allotted 15 minutes. Warn them that the participants tend to become very stressed if they are denied the opportunity to reach closure with their construction project. Ask for and respond to any questions from the volunteers.
(2 minutes.)

10. Explain the role of the Observer and read through that briefing sheet. Point out that the briefing sheet questions reflect the Project Planning sheet, so their job is to observe and assess the effectiveness of the Project Leader's project planning and leadership style. Remind them that they must stay silent throughout the activity, but they will be expected to provide a brief, non-judgmental summary of their observations. Say that humor is encouraged. Emphasize that their job is not to tear anyone down or to hurt anyone's feelings, but instead to provide objective, fact-based feedback. Ask for and respond to any questions.
(2 minutes.)

11. Return to the room, ask the volunteers to join their groups, and give the go-ahead to start, reminding the groups that they have only 15 minutes to complete their projects.

12. Observe the process, moving around the room to quietly encourage or acknowledge the activities of the Voices of Reality and the Observers. Serve as the timekeeper, alerting the groups when they have 10 minutes left, 5 minutes left, and 1 minute left. Make sure that the Voices of Reality cease obstructing the construction process by the 5-minute mark so that the groups can actually complete their merry-go-rounds.
(15 minutes.)

13. After stopping the process, hand out the Project Summary sheets and ask the participants who were involved in constructing the merry-go-rounds to complete them individually.
(3 minutes.)

14. Ask the Observers to use this time to plan their brief feedback reports to the entire group.

15. Allow each Observer approximately 3 minutes to provide feedback, reminding them before they begin of their responsibility to provide helpful, nonjudgmental feedback.
(10 to 15 minutes.)

16. Bring closure by facilitating a directed large group discussion of the participants' responses to each of the questions on the Merry-Go-Round Project Summary sheet. Ask additional questions, as relevant:

   - To what degree did each team member's own idea of how to organize and implement the project either assist with or detract from the Project Leader's vision and plan?

   - What options and alternatives do teams have when faced with the obstacles, interruptions, and challenges that occur daily to impede their progress?

   - How important was the planning process to the effective completion of the project?

   - How often do we take the time to plan properly before we begin a project? How does that affect the result?

   - How often do we consider the importance of gaining the buy-in of the team members and actually take some action to achieve that buy-in?

   - How often are project teams thrown together without regard to background, experience, or capability to actually perform the project work? What can you do differently back on the job?

   - What key learning are you taking from this experience?
   (30 minutes.)

Variations

- With groups of 5 or 6 per table, reduce the number of participants actually involved in the construction of the merry-go-round. Retain 1 Voice of Reality and 1 Observer for each table.

- With table groups of more than 7, increase the number of participants actually involved in the construction of the merry-go-round and/or add 1 more Voice of Reality (who might impose obstructions created by a regulatory agency or some other entity).

- To increase complexity, incorporate specific personality traits, work habits, motivations, and behavioral issues that are typical to the participants' workplace into roles assigned to the participants involved in the construction of the merry-go-round.

Submitted by Deborah Spring Laurel.

Deborah Spring Laurel, *president of Laurel and Associates, Ltd., is an international management training consultant who specializes in the design and presentation of skill building, participant centered workshops in personnel management, interpersonal relations, leadership, organization development, and train-the-trainer. She is also a Certified Professional Consultant to Management, with expertise in human resource management, organization development, and performance consulting. She has her master's degree from the University of Wisconsin-Madison.*

Merry-Go-Round Project Background Information

Situation

Organization X has successfully marketed a brand new product: a high quality, attractive, and affordable merry-go-round that is now small enough to be safely installed in urban parks, playgrounds, and even residential yards.

As a matter of fact, the marketing has been so successful that consumer demand has far exceeded the supply of available merry-go-rounds. Organization X needs to increase productivity to fill the current backorders.

However, since Organization X has sunk all of its available cash into marketing and inventory, it is not in a position to hire additional workers. Instead, the company has been forced to re-deploy workers from all of its other departments. None of these workers has ever worked on this merry-go-round project before.

Challenge

Your project team will be responsible for making a Tinkertoy merry-go-round that meets all engineering, quality, and OSHA requirements within 15 minutes.

There are 5 participants on each team. In addition, there are 2 other individuals involved with each team with special roles.

They will be responsible, respectively, for making this activity as realistic as possible by posing the types of challenges that teams typically experience and for silently observing the process and then reporting to the entire group at the end of the activity.

Merry-Go-Round Project Planning

The Project Leader is responsible for ensuring that the project team constructs a functioning Tinkertoy merry-go-round within 15 minutes despite the challenges that teams typically experience.

Assume that you will be the Project Leader and take 10 minutes to plan out the project before it begins:

1. What are the specific tasks that need to be done?

2. How will the work be divided among the team members?

3. How will you obtain the team's commitment to the project?

4. What information does the team need so that this project will run smoothly?

5. How will you manage the project to ensure that the construction process is successful?

6. What will your involvement be in the actual construction process?

7. What are the most probable challenges that may affect project completion?

8. How will you handle these challenges so that the project can continue?

9. How will you ensure that the project is completed on time?

10. Is there any other information that you need?

Merry-Go-Round Project Construction Instructions

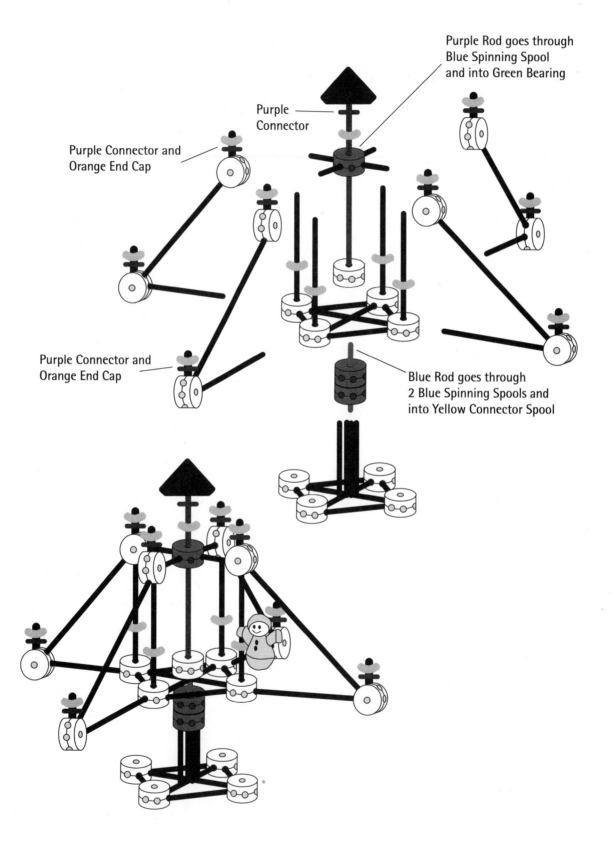

Purple Rod goes through
Blue Spinning Spool
and into Green Bearing

Purple
Connector

Purple Connector and
Orange End Cap

Purple Connector and
Orange End Cap

Blue Rod goes through
2 Blue Spinning Spools and
into Yellow Connector Spool

Merry-Go-Round Project Observer Briefing

You are expected to

- Quietly observe the project in progress;

- Answer the questions below; and

- Report your observations to the larger group in a *helpful, non-judgmental* manner.

1. How did the project leader obtain the team's commitment to the project?

2. What information did the project leader give the team so that this project would run smoothly?

3. How was the work divided among the team members?

4. What was the project leader's involvement in the actual construction process?

5. How did the project leader manage the project team?

6. How did the project leader maintain team commitment to the success of the project?

7. How did the team members work together to accomplish the goal?

8. How did the project leader handle interference?

9. How did the team members handle interference?

10. How did the project manager ensure that the project was completed on time?

11. How did the project team complete the task?

12. Did the team build the merry-go-round properly?

13. Does it function?

14. Would you purchase or ride on the merry-go-round?

15. Other observations or comments.

Merry-Go-Round Project Voice of Reality Briefing

You are responsible for making this activity as realistic as possible by posing the challenges that the teams in your organization typically experience. You will need to be creative. For example, consider the following distractions:

Lack of Staff

- Pull one member off the project for personal illness or a family emergency.

Policy Makers

- Tell them that they cannot use any green pieces. Then a couple of minutes later, tell them they can.

Standards

- Tell them that all of the connectors need to be washed, so they must remove them and wipe them down.

Lack of Resources

- Simply remove some pieces that they need. You can return them later, or not, as you wish.

Regulations

- Impose some restriction on them. For example, say, "Sorry, but you can only use your left hand to put on that kind of piece."

Miscommunication

- Give them misleading instructions. For example, say, "Two of you will need to work with your eyes closed" or "I'm sorry, but we'll need that completed in the next 5 minutes." You can correct your communication later, if you want.

Lack of Skill

- Find out who is spatially challenged and insist that this person be in charge of the more technical work.

Have fun with it, but try to keep your negative impact on the project realistic, relative to the 15-minute time frame. We will enroll you in a witness protection program after the exercise!

Merry-Go-Round Project Summary

Instructions: Fill out the answers to the questions below in preparation for a group discussion.

1. How did this experience feel?

2. How realistic was this experience compared with your actual workplace?

3. What strategies or emotions did it raise in you?

4. What did the project leader do well?

5. What could the project leader have done differently?

6. What can you take from this experience to apply to a current workplace team?

Search and Find:
Discovering Expertise and Sharing Information

Activity Summary

A highly interactive activity used to gather a large amount of information from individuals in a short amount of time.

Goal

- To identify the variety of expertise among team or group members.

Group Size

20 to 150 participants from the same organization, department, or work group.

Time Required

1 to 3 hours, depending on the number of topics covered and number of rounds. Plan at least 30 minutes per round.

Materials

- Newsprint sheets, one per topic to be discussed.

- Felt-tipped markers.

- Masking tape.

- A timer.

- Topic tent cards for each table.

Physical Setting

A room large enough to post newsprint charts around the room, with tables set up to accommodate small groups. (Round tables are the best, with seating for 8 to 10 per table.)

Facilitating Risk Rating

Moderate.

Preparation

1. Identify ahead of time the topics you want the group to discuss. For example, you may be conducting an Association Leadership Conference and want to discuss five topics: conducting board meetings; fund raising; succession planning; membership; and volunteer motivation.

2. Create one flip-chart sheet and one tent card for each topic. At the top of each chart, write the topic. Then list numbers down the side of the page to match the maximum number of people you want for each group. Draw lines horizontally across the page to separate the numbers. To determine how many horizontal sign-up lines you will have, take the number of people in the group, multiply by the number of rounds, and then divide by the number of topics. For example, 20 people times 3 rounds is 60. Divide 60 by 5 topics, which is 12 horizontal sign-up lines per topic.

3. On the right-hand side of each sheet, create two narrow columns: "Expert" and "Seeker," divided by a vertical line drawn between the headings, as shown in the two examples below.

Effective Board Meetings	Expert	Seeker
1.		
2.		
3.		
4.		
5.		
6.		
7.		
8.		
9.		
10.		
11.		
12.		

Fund Raising	Expert	Seeker
1.		
2.		
3.		
4.		
5.		
6.		
7.		
8.		
9.		
10.		
11.		
12.		

4. Post the charts around the room, each near a table.

5. Place one topic tent card on each table that is the same as the topic on the newsprint sheet hanging nearby.

Process

1. Begin by asking the group:

   "Have you ever noticed how often we overlook the expertise that we have right here within our group? Think about that old saying: 'Prophets in their own land are never valued.' We want to smash that stereotype today by scheduling time to do two things. First, we are going to find out who the experts in our group are, related to several specific topics. Then we are going to take some time to learn from those experts and gather ideas we can put into practice immediately back on the job. Trust me when I say that we all can fill the role of expert in some areas, while in other areas we seek information. This activity will allow you to do both."

   (3 minutes.)

2. Give the following directions:

   "Look around the room at the various topics we plan to discuss today. Our goal is to generate as many great ideas on each topic as we can in the time we have. Let's quickly identify the topics."

3. Now define each of the topics so that everyone is clear what it means. Then continue by saying:

   "Think for a moment about any of these areas in which you might be considered an 'expert.' Being an expert means you have experience in the area and have some ideas that you would comfortably share with others. Also think about in which topics you would consider yourself a 'seeker,' meaning that you would be interested in gaining more information and ideas about the topic so you could apply them in your work/life."

   (10 minutes.)

4. Continue by saying:

   "You will have an opportunity to sign up for [the number of rounds you are having] rounds of discussion. At one table you may be an 'expert' and at another you may be a 'seeker.' The decision is yours. However, I encourage you to try to see yourself in both roles for each topic. All of us have expertise to share, and all of us have things we can learn!

   "You will have 10 minutes to sign up for the [number of topics] topics you want. Simply write your name on the list under the topic you choose and check whether you are coming to that table as an expert or a seeker. Take a look at the chart as you sign up. If you notice an overload of experts and you had planned to sign on as an expert, you may want to choose another category. Once the list is full, that table is closed, and you must select another option. Remember, you are signing up for [the number of rounds you have selected] rounds."

5. Respond to any clarifying questions from the group, then allow 10 minutes for participants to sign up. (*Note:* You may find it useful to combine this with a break, if it fits in with your time schedule, so that no one feels rushed and no one becomes bored waiting for others to finish.) *(15 minutes.)*

6. Once everyone has reconvened, give the following instructions:

   "When we start, I would like everyone to go to one of the tables you chose. Each round will last for 20 minutes. Discussion will occur in the following format: 10 minutes for experts to share their ideas and respond to clarifying questions; 10 minutes for seekers to ask specific questions about the table topic and for general discussion about the topic."

   Say that you will give a 10-minute notice, and a 2-minute warning and that, when the time is up, everyone will move to a second topic table.

7. Have participants move to one of their choices. Due to the flexibility of choice, some tables may be empty for one of the rounds, since all those interested may select it during another round. Some groups may be very large and some small. If only one person is at a table, suggest that the person move to another one of his or her choices.

8. During the topic discussions, facilitate the process by wandering around, ensuring that no expert is dominating and that seekers have the opportunity to participate in the discussion. Give a 10-minute notice and a 2-minute warning.
   (20 minutes.)

9. After 20 minutes, instruct participants to move to another table for the next round. If there is a large group at one table and/or a lot of topics, you may want to remind people of where each topic is located.

10. Repeat the process for the number of rounds you have chosen. Call a quick stretch break and allow everyone to return to his or her original place.

11. The debriefing is critical to this exercise. Conduct a 60-second recap, which allows anyone to share a great idea he or she learned during the process. Say that no one is allowed more than 60 seconds to share an idea.
    (About 1 minute per participant.)

12. Reinforce the benefits of the activity and bring closure using your choice of the following questions:

- What have you learned about the expertise within our group?

- What common themes did you hear?

- What are some changes you want to make as a result of what you found out during this activity?

- How did you feel about sharing your ideas as an expert with other members of this team? How did you feel in the role of seeker?

- How can we take advantage of the ideas that we have generated during this activity when we return to the job?

(10 minutes.)

Variations

- Prior to the session, select a "host" for each table to serve as facilitator of the process. This individual can also take responsibility for capturing the ideas so they can be typed and shared with everyone at a later time.

- Prior to the session, identify a "resident expert" for each topic to ensure that each table has an expert. Charge that person with being prepared to share a powerful idea/technique/strategy to kick off the discussion at that table.

- For a very large group, assign more than one table for the same topic.

- Instead of using predetermined topics, simply post charts prepared the same way, minus the topics. Then have participants create their own desired topics prior to signing up.

Submitted by Cher Holton.

Cher Holton, Ph.D., *president of The Holton Consulting Group, Inc., is an impact consultant focusing on rekindling the human spirit. She is a Certified Speaking Professional and Certified Management Consultant and is author of* The Manager's Short Course to a Long Career; Living at the Speed of Life: Staying in Control in a World Gone Bonkers!; Suppose. . .Questions to Turbo-Charge Your Business and Your Life; *and* From Ballroom to Bottom Line. . .in Business and in Life.

Hubris: Eliminating the Personal Delusion of Arrogance

Activity Summary

This activity was designed to assist executives with the condition of hubris.

Goals

- To help executive-level managers understand and appreciate the concept of hubris.

- To provide an assessment of individual levels of hubris.

- To create a safe environment for individuals to discuss hubris and what they can do to change their own behavior.

Trainer Note

It is unlikely that a training or development program dedicated solely to the problem of hubris could be effectively launched. After all, who would pay for it and who would attend? What can be done, however, is to include the topic as an integral part of any executive development program by either creating a short module that deals with the information presented here, supported by some interactive exercise, or, after introducing the concept of hubris, to use this activity as one means of processing all other content modules in the program. If you do not introduce and emphasize this problem as an inherent pitfall in all executive success, it isn't going to surface.

The challenge is, first, to make the executives aware of the nature of hubris and, second, to give them an opportunity to avoid it or confront it in a safe and image-protecting environment. The neutrality of the training/development milieu can provide such a setting.

This exercise uses the value of humor and learning from past error to make positive behavioral changes with regard to arrogance. The objective is to get the participants to laugh at themselves and at some of their own foibles.

Group Size

As many as 24 executives divided into 6 subgroups.

Time Required

Approximately 2.5 hours.

Materials

- One copy of the Hubris: I'm Not Perfect handout for each participant.
- One copy of the Hubris Self-Image Analyzer for each participant.
- One copy of the Hubris Scoring Interpretation for each participant.
- One copy of Hubris: Executive Widow Maker article for each participant.
- Pens or pencils for participants.
- Flip chart and markers.
- Masking tape.
- (Optional) A supply of gag prizes.

Physical Setting

A room that is large enough to accommodate 4 to 6 subgroups so that they do not disturb each other as they discuss sensitive personal issues.

Facilitating Risk Rating

Moderate to high.

Process

1. Introduce the activity, pointing out that the purpose is to relax and get to know each other from a different perspective while they learn about their own behavior. Explain the goals and show the participants the "trophies" that the winners will receive (if you are using prizes).

2. Give one copy of the Hubris: I'm Not Perfect handout and a pen or pencil to each participant and tell the group that their lists do not have to be work-related and they can come from childhood as easily as from last week. Say that they will have 15 minutes to complete their worksheets in silence. *(15 minutes.)*

3. When everyone has finished, ask them to form 6 small groups and to share their lists within their groups. Tell them that they should select a "winning" item from each list, based on the humor of the situation either at the time or in retrospect. *(10 minutes.)*

4. Now ask each "winner" to stand up and *brag* about the incident to the total group. *(1 minute per person.)*

5. Have the total group vote on the best incident in each category by a show of hands and present the winner of each category with a small gag prize (if you have chosen to do this).

6. Lead a discussion on the learning deriving from the exercise. If the group or anyone in it has found this difficult to do, explore the dangers implicit in taking oneself too seriously or the costs inherent in losing one's sense of humor. If participants have had a good time doing this, ask if this represents a reasonable view to what their work life is like. If not, process why not, and what they might be able to do to get more laughter into their work. Also ask these questions:

   • How competitive were you in trying to win the "prize" or to be voted the best?

   • What are the implications to bringing humor to some serious topics?

   • Do you view each other any differently as a result of having gone through this exercise together? (Direct all feedback to the individuals for whom it is intended.)
   (15 minutes.)

7. Make the point that while all/most of the participants are observably successful today, they did not start out that way. Their present level of success is partially due to past risk taking and/or surviving and learning from failure. Ask whether they are still willing to take risks and be vulnerable to making mistakes. Segue into the topic of how they may have been affected by their success, by the organization's culture, and by trying to preserve their own self-images.

8. Provide copies of the Hubris Self-Image Analyzer and ask them to complete it individually to ascertain how they view their present levels of confidence and success. Tell them to also complete the scoring portion of the analyzer. *(15 minutes.)*

9. Once they have finished, distribute copies of the Hubris Scoring Interpretation to each person and ask them to read through it. Then have them show by raised hands how many fell into each category. (Note that this option should not be used if there is any reasonable risk of embarrassing a participant. However, as participants know one another, they presumably would not be surprised by others' scores.) *(30 minutes.)*

10. Introduce the concept of hubris by handing out the Hubris: Executive Widow Maker article and having them read it in silence. *(5 minutes.)*

11. Have them form once again into 6 small groups and discuss how the content of the article is relative to themselves or to their organization. After about 15 minutes, pull the group together for a discussion of problems inherent in hubris. Discuss this topic without making any implications about the participants or anyone they know. Point out that hubris is a "disease" of the highly successful! *(20 minutes.)*

12. Conclude by asking each participant to make a single statement to the group about what he or she gained most from the session. Post these on the flip chart. Ask what they intend to do differently in the future as a result of what they have learned about themselves.

Submitted by H.B. Karp

H.B. Karp, Ph.D., *is an associate professor of management at Christopher Newport University in Newport News, Virginia. He is also the owner of Personal Growth Systems, a management consulting firm in Chesapeake, Virginia. He consults with a variety of Fortune 500 and government organizations in the areas of leadership development, team building, conflict management, and executive coaching. He specializes in applying Gestalt theory to issues of individual growth and organizational effectiveness. He is the author of many articles and has written several books, including* Personal Power: An Unorthodox Guide to Success *and* The Change Leader: Using a Gestalt Approach with Work Groups, *and has most recently co-authored,* Bridging the Boomer-Xer Gap: Creating Authentic Teams for High Performance at Work.

Hubris: I'm Not Perfect

My Personally Most Embarrassing Moment

Instructions: While screw-ups usually occur in the process of trying to accomplish something, the threat of embarrassment lurks virtually everywhere. These events are most often of our own creation; however, many of them are suffered at the well-meaning hands of our parents, relatives, close friends and colleagues. Regardless of the source, think of a time when, if you had had a choice, death would have been preferable to enduring the 5 minutes that followed the incident. Again, it has to be something that, while extremely painful at the time, now brings a chuckle with the memory.

What happened?

What did you learn about yourself?

If I Could Go Back in Time and Fix One Thing

Instructions: As with screw-ups and embarrassing moments, most of us have a few regrets that we bring along with us. These are rarely humorous, because frequently these events have a load of guilt attached to them. Sometimes, in just stating them out loud, you give yourself permission to finally set the burden down. What regret are you carrying with you that, if you could fix it, you would? Choose something that is okay to surface with the group.

What was the mistake?

What were the effects?

How would you fix it, if you could?

Screw-Ups That Nobody Knows But Me

Instructions: All of us, at one time or another, have really messed up. Usually we were discovered and then had to pay the price by enduring the accompanying embarrassment and loss of self-image. We survived these faux pas, learned from them (we hope), and then moved on to our next one. Every once in a while, however, we catch a break. We screw up and actually get away with it.

In the space below, think back to your childhood, your college years, your early work life, or last week. See whether you can recall a few of your more creative mistakes in judgment that no one found out about. Look for things that, while devastating then, bring forth a low-grade chuckle now that you recall them. Choose only incidents that you are comfortable sharing with the group. Provide some detail as to what happened, how you got away with it, and what, if anything, you learned.

Event 1

What did you learn?

Event 2

What did you learn?

Hubris Self-Image Analyzer

Instructions: Please respond to each statement below as honestly as you can. No one will see your answers if you don't wish to share them. It is important that each response reflect how *you* feel about each statement, *right now, at this time in your life and career.* Remember that there are no right or wrong answers, nor are there any preferred answers to any statement.

SD = Strongly Disagree   D = Disagree   DS = Disagree Somewhat   N = Neutral
AS = Agree Somewhat   A = Agree   SA = Strongly Agree

1. Things are going really well for me now and have been for some time.   SD   D   DS   N   AS   A   SA

2. Almost all the feedback I receive from others is highly positive.   SD   D   DS   N   AS   A   SA

3. My current level of success can really be attributed to pure luck.   SD   D   DS   N   AS   A   SA

4. My views are highly sought by others.   SD   D   DS   N   AS   A   SA

5. When others have disdgreed with me, it usually has turned out that I was correct.   SD   D   DS   N   AS   A   SA

6. One of my main missions is to empower those below me.   SD   D   DS   N   AS   A   SA

7. Right now, I think I could take on the world.   SD   D   DS   N   AS   A   SA

8. I get little satisfaction out of being proven right.   SD   D   DS   N   AS   A   SA

9. I am receiving the high level of recognition from others that I genuinely deserve.   SD   D   DS   N   AS   A   SA

10. While others seem to really value my contributions, I know that I'm a fraud and that I'm going to be caught one of these days.   SD   D   DS   N   AS   A   SA

SD = Strongly Disagree   D = Disagree   DS = Disagree Somewhat   N = Neutral
AS = Agree Somewhat   A = Agree   SA = Strongly Agree

11. My position in the organization is so solid at present that there is little chance that anyone could do me any real harm.   SD   D   DS   N   AS   A   SA

12. My working relationships with those whom I hold in high regard seem to be a little strained right now.   SD   D   DS   N   AS   A   SA

13. I have little sense of which way the political winds are blowing in my organization.   SD   D   DS   N   AS   A   SA

14. My contribution and/or views are becoming increasingly valued by those with whom I have an indirect working relationship.   SD   D   DS   N   AS   A   SA

15. I am slowly becoming a force to be reckoned with in my field of expertise.   SD   D   DS   N   AS   A   SA

Scoring

With the exception of items 3, 8, 10, and 13, the items are scored as follows:

	Points
Strongly Disagree	1
Disagree	2
Agree Somewhat	3
Neutral	4
Agree Somewhat	5
Agree	6
Strongly Agree	7

For items 3, 8,10, and 13, score as follows:

	Points
Strongly Disagree	7
Disagree	6
Agree Somewhat	5
Neutral	4
Agree Somewhat	3
Agree	2
Strongly Agree	1

Find the point value for each of the 15 items and then sum them for a total score.

Total Survey Score: _____

Hubris Scoring Interpretation

The intention of this survey was to alert you to the possibility that your self-image may not be reflective of what is actually occurring on the job. That is, a relatively low score could indicate that things are not going very well for you at the present time or it could indicate that you are underestimating your impact on, and your contribution to, the organization.

A relatively high score could reflect reality, or it could be that you are vastly over-estimating your present worth to the system and how you are being seen. Think of the survey as a "flashing red light." The intent is to have you stop, look around carefully, and then proceed with caution.

Second, this survey is not intended to be predictive, or even descriptive, in nature. It's sole intent is to have you look at your score, examine the individual items that contributed to it, and then determine whether the information reflects reality or a distorted self-image. You can certainly discuss the results with others to hear their perceptions; however, only you can determine which interpretation is valid.

If your score falls between 15 and 44, there is a reasonable possibility that you are underestimating your worth and contribution to the organization. There are many causes for this phenomenon, and they are widespread. Probably the major contributing cause is carrying messages from our formative years. As parents, teachers, clergy, and others attempt to civilize us, they also inadvertently send a message that "You should always discount your own worth."

Adult directives such as, "Always be humble," "Never brag," "Always put others first," "The majority rules," ad nauseam, are not bad things, in and of themselves. The bad thing is the "always" or "never" lead-ins. If a child is receiving only these messages, the unavoidable result will be a diminishing of the self and a discounting of what one has accomplished because it did not include others' feelings or respect for parental messages.

A second cause for consistently discounting one's efforts and impact is failing to obtain, or even ask for, feedback. Sometimes it takes others' perspectives to enlighten us or to reinforce our own perceptions of our effectiveness. Managers who fall into this range tend to take fewer real risks for fear of failing and being discovered as less effective than others credit them for being. Underestimating personal effectiveness, however, is not usually the problem with people at your level of the organization.

If your score falls between 45 and 74, chances are that you have a good grip on how your career is developing. Those falling in this range possess a healthy amount of self-confidence and know how their efforts contribute to the organization's objectives. While recognizing their worth to the system, these managers are also aware that they do make errors from time to time and can learn from them. They take satisfaction from accomplishment and enjoy the recognition from others that usually accompanies it. They also recognize that each accomplishment has its own half-life and that the next challenge coming down will have its own probabilities for success or failure. They are willing to take on most well-thought-out, well-grounded risks. Most manager/executives who are continuing to grow and advance tend to fall within this range.

If your score falls between 75 and 105, you could be heading into the dangerous area of overestimating the value of your contribution and your worth to the organization. Those scoring in this range, while quite effective, tend to focus only on their successes and the praise that accompanies them. The appreciation of others becomes the main criterion by which they measure their own worth, which can have an almost narcotic effect. While the successes are genuine and the appreciation appropriate, any information that counters the self-image of "conqueror" is increasingly avoided or discounted. Managers and executives who fall into this range are usually willing to take on any risk, since they see themselves as destined for success and invulnerable, regardless of what other indicators might be out there. This condition goes by the term "hubris" and is frequently a chronic illness of the successful.

If your score reflects reality as you see it, fine. This is good to know and should point out areas that can aid you in becoming more effective. If, on the other hand, the score does not seem to reflect reality, then you may wish to discuss with others how they see you and your contributions to the organization.

Hubris: Executive Widow Maker

Since the dawn of civilization there have been more leaders brought down by hubris than by swords, plots, or any other method of removing people from executive positions. Hubris, which is simply defined as "arrogance" or "excessive pride" in the *Random House Dictionary* is much more than this, and certainly much more devastating. To begin with, we need a comprehensive and descriptive definition of this phenomenon. To that end let me offer the following: Hubris is deepening a sense of well-being and pride that grows into a delusion of invulnerability and total control over one's environment.

The Origin and Nature of Hubris

Hubris shares some of the dynamics of groupthink (Janis, 1973), but groupthink is a group dynamic, whereas hubris is strictly an individual phenomenon. Hubris has several sources. First, hubris is the result of receiving massive amounts of positive feedback and nothing else. The fact that the feedback is accurate and that it may even be universal only makes the matter worse. Regardless of how effective a manager really is, there is always room for growth, along with a range of opinions about just how good that manager really is. To lose sight of this variance and focus only on the best possible interpretation sets one up for a disastrous comedown.

For a more in-depth and comprehensive discussion of hubris see Karp and Jackson's *Hubris: A Gestalt Alternative to Groupthink"* (in press).

Two conditions must exist for hubris to occur: (1) performance must be subjectively measured and (2) performance must have direct impact on the lives and/or the well-being of others. For example, careers subject to hubris would be managers, professors, actors, clergy, university presidents, and consultants. Careers not subject to hubris would be professional athletes, tool and dye makers, engineers, sales reps, and certified public accountants.

Hubris is a quantitative condition. It operates much like any other quantitative attribute, for example, body temperature. To illustrate, good health requires a body temperature of something around 98.6 degrees. When the body becomes ill, the temperature increases and, as it rises, "temperature" becomes "fever." Hubris operates the same way psychologically. Attributes such as confidence, pride in accomplishment, and self-esteem are critical to one's continued success and sense of well-being. As these attributes increase, a healthy threshold is eventually reached. If the attribute, for example, self-confidence, increases past this point, hubris begins to emerge and takes an increasingly firmer grip on one's perceptions. If left unchecked, it will eventually evolve into a highly toxic form of self-delusion. One might say that hubris is the classic example of "way too much of a good thing."

The Symptoms of Hubris

Hubris has eight symptoms:

1. The myth of invulnerability;

2. The myth of omnipotence;

3. A belief in one's press;

4. Seeing oneself as "messianic";

5. Believing that one is infallible;

6. Interpreting external dissension as ignorance;

7. Being previously misunderstood or discounted; and

8. Believing that one can "empower" others.

Countering Hubris

Although hubris can be seen as the "silent killer," there are several things that you can do to reverse its effects or avoid them altogether. These are

1. Check to see whether things have been going too well for too long;

2. Note whether close friends or colleagues seem somewhat less comfortable around you than previously;

3. Ask for corrective, as well as supportive feedback;

4. Make a point of assisting others in gaining their objectives;

5. Give as much credit as you can to those who have contributed to your successes;

6. Learn to laugh at yourself; and

7. Introduce this topic as an integral part of any executive development program.

Conclusion

Hubris is a problem that has been plaguing leaders down through the millennia. The bad news is that there is no way to avoid the probability that it will accompany any sustained period of success. The good news is that you can defeat it through awareness and a willingness to confront it. If things have been going too well for too long, be afraid, be very afraid. Then check it out.

References

Janis, I. L. (1973). *Victims of groupthink: A psychological study of foreign policy decisions and fiascoes.* New York: Houghton Mifflin.

Karp, H. B., & Jackson, K. L. (2004). *Hubris: A gestalt alternative to groupthink. Gestalt Review, 8* (1).

Mentor:
Defining the Role

Activity Summary

An activity that helps participants understand the concept of mentoring.

Goals

- To develop a working definition of a mentor.

- To review what a mentor is and what a mentor is not.

Group Size

10 to 20 participants who may be candidates for a mentoring program.

Time Required

60 to 80 minutes, depending on the number of subgroups. If participants are divided into two groups, the activity will take approximately 60 minutes; if there are four groups, 80 minutes.

Materials

- A flip-chart sheet, prepared in advance, with the heading "Mentor Wanted" for each subgroup.

- A flip-chart sheet, prepared in advance, with "A Mentor Is/Is Not" written on it for each subgroup.

- One copy of the Mentor Want Ad Assignments for each subgroup (or use an overhead transparency, if desired).

- One copy of the Mentor Definitions Sheet for each participant.

- One copy of the A Mentor Is/Is Not Handout for each participant.
- A flip chart with plenty of paper.
- Felt-tipped markers in a variety of colors for the subgroups.
- Masking tape.
- Blank paper and pens or pencils for participants.
- (Optional) An overhead projector.

Physical Setting

A room in which flip-chart sheets can be posted on the wall and several sub-groups can meet simultaneously without disturbing one another.

Facilitating Risk Rating

Moderate.

Process

1. Introduce the activity by briefly talking about some of your personal experiences as a mentor or as someone who has been mentored. Ask the participants about their organizations' current mentoring programs (formal or informal) or planned or hoped-for mentoring programs.
   (5 minutes.)

2. Divide the participants into 2 (optional: 3 or 4) groups. Small groups of 4 to 5 members work best. Give each participant a sheet of blank paper and a pen or pencil. Give the groups the prepared Mentor Wanted flip chart sheets and copies of the Mentor Want Ad Assignments sheet. Read through the assignments, clarifying as necessary.

3. Provide each subgroup with markers, telling them they will be expected to present their "want ads" to the large group in 10 minutes.
   (10 minutes.)

4. Ask the groups to stop and prepare to report out. After the presentations, ask the participants to return to their subgroups. Based on the two (or four) want ads they have heard, ask them to develop a single definition of the word "mentor." Provide each group with one of the prepared flip chart sheets titled "A Mentor Is/Is Not" and ask them to complete it by defining a mentor to the best of their ability.
   (10 minutes.)

5. Ask all the groups to post their final definitions simultaneously on the wall using masking tape. Comment on the similarities and differences among the definitions. Lead a discussion focused on the characteristics they have defined, reaching a group consensus on what should be on the final sheet. *(10 minutes.)*

6. Then provide each participant with a copy of the Mentor Definitions Sheet and tell everyone that these are the definitions that you will be using when discussing mentors. Read the definitions to the participants and answer any questions. *(10 minutes.)*

7. Review the Mentor Is/Is Not flip chart sheets that the groups prepared earlier, noting the items you consider especially important to the participants, based on what they said during their presentations to the group and the definitions you have just discussed. Post these on a flip chart. Clarify as needed and then distribute the Mentor Is/Is Not Handout for the participants to use as a reference. *(10 minutes.)*

8. Summarize the activity with the following questions:

   • Has this activity changed your ideas of what a mentor is? In what way?

   • Do you view a person who is being mentored differently as a result of our discussion? In what way?

   • Will you change your own style when you are a mentor in the future? In what way?

   • How do you think that your mentoring style relates to your leadership style?

   • What changes will you make on the job as a mentor or a mentoree as a result of what you have learned here? *(10 minutes.)*

9. Close the activity by reminding participants that mentoring does not require someone to "be all things" to the person being mentored; however, it does require an agreement between the mentor and the person being mentored, with responsibilities being met by both parties.

Variations

- When the definitions of a mentor are posted by the different groups, group members may trade and circulate them, rather than post them on the wall. Once everyone has had an opportunity to review other definitions, the groups may re-form to revise their definitions before the final report.

- Ask the participants to review the Mentor Is/Is Not Handout and make additions based on their experience and/or organization's culture.

- Tailor the Mentor Is/Is Not Handout ahead of time based on the organization's culture.

- Add the organization's definition of a mentor to the Mentor Definitions Sheet.

Submitted by Betsy Kendall and Mardy Wheeler.

Betsy Kendall *is a principal of Kendall & Wheeler, a firm specializing in the design of training programs for business, industry, social service, government, and academic institutions. In addition, she is an adjunct faculty member for the University of New Hampshire.*

Mardy Wheeler *is a principal of Kendall & Wheeler, a firm specializing in the design of training programs for business, industry, social service, government, and academic institutions. In addition, she is a member of the adjunct faculty for the University of New Hampshire.*

Mentor Want Ad Assignments

Group 1

Wanted—a mentor who (from the view of a person being mentored)

Group 2

Wanted—someone to mentor who (from the view of a mentor)

Group 3

Wanted—a mentoring program that will (from the view of the organization)

Group 4

Wanted—a mentoring program that will (from the view of the organization's customers)

Mentor Definitions Sheet

Mentor as Colleague. A colleague who is prepared to listen, provide feedback and encouragement, suggest options, and maintain focus on the task at hand.

Mentor as Teacher. An expert in a particular content area or areas who is prepared to share his or her knowledge in a systematic way, transmitting knowledge and "testing" for understanding.

Mentor as Facilitator. A trainer who concentrates on creating and maintaining a climate in which the trainee can be responsible for his or her own learning; ties models and theories with real-world application.

Mentor as Coach. A pragmatist who watches the trainee practice, gives feedback, and redirects efforts.

A Mentor Is/Is Not Handout

A Mentor Is	Is Not
• Prepared to practice the Four-Step Method: (1) state the task; (2) show and tell; (3) try it out; (4) follow up at decreasing intervals	• Expected to be perfect
• Prepared to discuss outcomes of training sessions with the colleague as soon as appropriate	• Expected to concentrate on the trainee when practice sessions include a customer
• A professional colleague	• A parent, a competitor, a baby-sitter, a manager
• Prepared to give feedback to the colleague's manager ONLY AFTER discussing it with the colleague	• Prepared to give feedback to the colleague's manager without discussing it first with the colleague
• A resource and a sounding board for the colleague	• A provider of all information to the colleague; possessor of all wisdom
• Accessible at scheduled times	• Accessible at the colleague's beck and call
• Allowed to have a sense of humor with the colleague and with the customers	• Allowed to poke fun at the colleague or at customers

Think Up the Organization:
Building Awareness of Top-Management Concerns

Activity Summary

This activity is designed to help participants become aware of issues that are important to higher levels of an organization.

Goals

- To raise awareness of the concerns and issues at higher levels of an organization.

- To consider broader definitions of success for higher organizational levels.

Group Size

20 to 30 participants from the same organization.

Time Required

90 minutes.

Materials

- A Think Up the Organization Personal Review handout for each participant.

- Copies of Think Up the Organization Management Review as needed.

- A pencil or pen for each participant.

- Blank paper for each participant.

- Flip chart and markers.

Physical Setting

One room with seating and writing surfaces for all.

Facilitating Risk Rating

Low.

Process

1. Explain the goals of this activity to the group. Ask participants whether they would think differently about organizational issues if they were in a higher position and ask what issues would concern them in that case. Post their ideas on the flip chart.
   (5 minutes.)

2. Say to the group:

   "Promotion to higher levels in an organization requires people to think differently from those who are in technical or functional areas. For example, how would you have to think differently if you managed your entire department? How would you measure success for the whole department? Would you look differently at the organization? How could you use these insights in your present role?"

3. Tell the participants they will first describe the responsibilities and then determine how they would define success for their own jobs and then come up with the same information for each level above them in the organization. Tell them to think about the various levels or departments of the organization above their positions—of the managers at each level above them (whether they know the person's name or not).

4. Distribute pens or pencils and copies of the handouts to all participants, one Think Up the Organization Personal Review for each person to fill out about himself or herself and one Think Up the Organization Management Review to fill out for each level of the organization above that person. (Note that there may be many levels or only one.) Tell them to write the key product or service responsibilities for their positions on their Personal Review sheets and to write a definition of success for their own level.
   (15 minutes.)

5. Now tell participants to write the key responsibilities for each higher level on their Management Review sheets. If they don't know something with certainty, tell them to take their best guesses. Also have them write their best guess definitions of success for those higher levels. (If someone is not sure,

ask him or her to consider first how failure might be indicated.) Tell them to repeat the process for each higher position, up to and including the chief executive officer (CEO).
(20 minutes.)

6. Bring the group together and lead a discussion about things they did not know about higher levels or departments. List these on a flip chart. *(15 minutes.)*

7. Have the group form dyads to identify people or resources to consult for further information. Give them blank paper and tell them to write down any new information they did not know that their partners revealed about particular positions or departments.
(10 minutes.)

8. Bring the whole group together to share their ideas and reactions. Summarize the activity by discussing the following questions:

   - Where in the organization can you learn more or discuss topics of broader concern or scope?

   - What professional or trade organizations could you join to learn more about your organization's place in the market?

   - What do you think is the definition of success for the organization as a whole?

   - What, if anything, will you do back on the job as a result of this activity?

   - Why will you do anything at all? (How might this affect your future career?)
   (20 minutes.)

9. Encourage the group to read books and articles or conduct informational interviews with people who occupy higher positions in the company.

Variation

- Invite management representatives or consultants to speak to the group.

Submitted by W. Norman Gustafson.

W. Norman Gustafson, M.S., *is a consultant and educator, teaching business and technology at the college and secondary level for eighteen years. He directs a training project at Fresno Pacific University and specializes in web-based training, performance improvement, and business model development. As a director, he is known for his board evaluation and development work. He has published a variety of consulting and training articles, including four in Pfeiffer's Annuals.*

Think Up the Organization Personal Review

Instructions: For your position in the organization, list your key responsibilities and the definition for your success below.

My position:

My key responsibilities (list the top three):

For my position, success is defined as:

Think Up the Organization Management Review

Instructions: Write the responsibilities and definitions of success for one of the levels above you.

Management position:

Position responsibilities:

For this level, success is defined as:

"Those Who Matter":
Group-Based Stakeholder Analysis

Activity Summary

An in-depth activity designed to assist an organization's senior leaders to create strategies to address external stakeholders.

Goals

- To assist participants in identifying their organization's most critical stakeholders and their expectations.

- To determine the type of influence stakeholders are likely to exercise on the organization.

- To help the participants formulate strategies to address potentially hostile stakeholders.

Group Size

3 to 4 subgroups of 5 to 6 corporate executives holding senior administrative positions, senior managers of a newly established organization, or senior managers of an organization that is restructuring (preferably with cross-functional responsibilities within the same organization).

Time Required

2 to 3 hours, but this activity may take more time, so be flexible.

Materials

- A copy of the "Those Who Matter" Lecturette for the facilitator.

- One copy of the "Those Who Matter" Stakeholder Categories on an overhead transparency or flip chart sheet (prepared in advance).

- A copy of "Those Who Matter" Individual Worksheet for each participant.

- A copy of "Those Who Matter" Generic Strategies for Dealing with Stakeholders for each participant.

- One copy of the "Those Who Matter" Group Worksheet for each of the stakeholders.

- Flip chart and markers.

- A loose sheet of flip-chart paper for each stakeholder who has been identified.

- Pencils and extra paper for all participants.

- Clip board or writing surface for the moderator of each subgroup.

- Pins or masking tape.

Physical Setting

A large room with adequate space for each subgroup to work without disturbing others. Movable chairs for each subgroup for the group activity.

Facilitating Risk Rating

Moderate to high.

Process

1. Welcome the participants and explain the goals of the activity. Give the "Those Who Matter" Lecturette and answer any questions. During the lecturette, post the "Those Who Matter" Stakeholder Categories sheet prepared previously. *(5 to 10 minutes.)*

2. Distribute the "Those Who Matter" Individual Worksheet and a pencil to each participant, review the instructions, answer any questions the participants may have, and allow them to complete the worksheet individually. *(10 to 20 minutes.)*

3. After the participants complete the "Those Who Matter" Individual Worksheet ask them to, one at a time, call out the stakeholders they have listed on their worksheets. Write the name of each stakeholder, his or her expectation(s), and the type of influence each exerts on a separate flip-chart sheet (one sheet for

each stakeholder). Encourage discussion among the participants to add to or modify the stakeholders' expectations and the type of influence that stakeholders exert. Do not list the same stakeholder more than once.
(15 to 20 minutes.)

4. Have participants assemble in 3 or 4 subgroups. Divide the list of stakeholders equally and assign the same number to each subgroup, either randomly or by choice (preferably not more than 6 stakeholders per subgroup). Do not assign the same stakeholder to more than one subgroup. Give the flip chart pages containing the stakeholder expectations to the respective subgroups, along with markers and masking tape or pins for posting them.
(5 minutes.)

5. Give everyone a copy of the "Those Who Matter" Generic Strategies for Dealing with Stakeholders and briefly discuss each one.
(5 minutes.)

6. Assign each subgroup a designated location in the room and tell subgroups to choose one of their members as a moderator.
(5 to 10 minutes.)

7. Distribute one copy of the "Those Who Matter" Group Worksheet to each subgroup for each of the stakeholders they have been assigned. Ask the subgroups to note the stakeholders assigned to them and the respective list of expectations from the flip-chart pages and then discuss the likely behavior (or the outcome) for each stakeholder, if his or her expectation(s) is not met by the organization. Tell them to note the stakeholder behavior/outcome in single statements. Explain that they may start from the most adverse/hostile behavior or outcome ("worst case" scenario) if they wish. Encourage the subgroups to brainstorm (a) why a stakeholder would take such an adversarial stand and (b) how the organization should respond to any such adverse-hostile reaction or behavior. While the participants discuss the organization's response strategy, remind them about the type of influence the stakeholders are capable of. The subgroups should note their response strategies directly on the worksheets.
(30 to 40 minutes.)

8. Reassemble the large group and ask someone from each subgroup to present that subgroup's view on why a stakeholder would become hostile and what response the organization should give in dealing with each hostile behavior or outcome. Guide the discussion among the participants on the appropriateness of or the likely impact of the response strategies.
(30 to 40 minutes.)

9. Summarize the discussion in terms of the various types of stakeholders and their expectations, varied behavior of the stakeholders, and the appropriateness of the response strategies that have been suggested. *(10 to 20 minutes.)*

10. Process this activity by asking the following questions:

    • How critical is it for your organization to be prepared for negative or hostile stakeholder behavior?

    • What have you learned during this session about your organization's response to stakeholder expectations?

    • What do you think your organization needs to do next?

    • What plans can you make now to be prepared for adverse stakeholder reactions in the future? *(5 to 10 minutes.)*

11. You may end the activity by suggesting that the participants form task forces or committees within the organization to develop standard guidelines and activity plans for dealing with different stakeholders. These guidelines may be based on the generic strategies identified during this session. Encourage them to set deadlines for developing these plans and to hold one another accountable.

Variations

• Prior to working in subgroups, participants may arrive at a group consensus on a limited number of stakeholders who are most crucial to the organization and then only discuss their expectations and suggest response strategies for this select list of stakeholders. This will shorten the time required.

• An overhead transparency of the "Those Who Matter" Stakeholder Management Strategies Group Worksheet could be used and the discussion summarized on this for better presentation and for wider discussion in the organization later.

• Participants could also be encouraged to discuss the organization's expectation(s) of the stakeholders.

• Hold a separate session on the expectations of the *internal* stakeholders and their likely behavior that should be planned for.

Submitted by A. Venkat Raman.

A. Venkat Raman *is a senior lecturer in the Faculty of Management Studies (FMS), University of Delhi. He teaches courses in human resource management and health care management. His training and consultancy interests include human resource planning, performance management, training needs assessment, and strategic analysis of health care organizations. He has conducted several training programs for senior executives of corporate hospitals, industrial establishments, and government departments. He was a recipient of the 2001 Robert McNamara fellowship of the World Bank.*

"Those Who Matter" Lecturette

At the end of this activity, you will know which stakeholders are most important to your organization and why. You will determine their expectations of your organization and how you can deal effectively with hostile stakeholders.

Stakeholders are individuals or groups (trustees, consumer groups, labor unions, professional associations) and/or institutions (competitors, media, government agencies, accreditation boards, financial institutions) who have significant direct or indirect influence over the way your organization functions and who help shape your policies, decisions, and actions.

Executives are responsible for managing a complex web of relationships with a number of powerful stakeholders every day. Stakeholders portend considerable potential for cooperation or conflict with the decisions and actions of the organization. Sometimes the potential for conflict could threaten the very survival of the organization. The objective of stakeholder analysis is to develop generic but robust management strategies to move a less favorable stakeholder into a more favorable category.

Stakeholders can be broadly categorized into *external, internal,* and *intermediary* stakeholders. While the management of internal stakeholders is dependent on the organizational policies and management systems, the most powerful stakeholders are external to the organization (Blair & Fottler, 1998) and the organization exerts little or no control over them.

The potential for conflict depends on three crucial factors, (1) the relative power of the stakeholder compared to the organization; (2) the nature of the issue; and (3) the degree of dependency on the stakeholder. Stakeholders tend to exhibit their power only when dealing with an issue of significance. The more the organization depends on the stakeholder's support, the more powerful the stakeholder becomes and the more conflict and potential for threat exist. The more dependent stakeholders are on the organization, the more support and cooperation they will tend to exhibit. Stakeholder power is manifest in the form of control of resources (funds, patients), ability to impose costs, and regulatory restrictions. The issues that confront both the organization and stakeholders are related to cost, quality, and access to services.

If organizational executives are to lead more effectively, they must determine the competing expectations of their stakeholders in the context of the relative influence these stakeholders possess and develop an integrated approach to managing their expectations. Rather than providing episodic responses from their functional areas, executives must evaluate the impact of every decision taken by the organization on stakeholder relationships (for example, acquiring more sophisticated technology could increase cost of goods).

In this session, you will visualise and respond to the "worst case" scenarios for stakeholder dissatisfaction and come up with pre-emptive strategies that will maximize the organization's effectiveness.

You will first identify all relevant external stakeholders, characterize the type of influence (power) each stakeholder may have over the organization, and then visualize each stakeholder's expectations from the organization. Next you will categorize the stakeholders according to their potential for cooperation or conflict, formulate generic stakeholder management strategies, and develop specific action plans and protocols for dealing with each stakeholder. While participating in this activity, be conscious of your own (or your organization's) biases so that nothing is overlooked, whether a potential for cooperation or for conflict.

It is important to remember that stakeholders do not necessarily react the way we want them to react. Stakeholder behavior could change depending on what the organization does or fails to do and on expectations around a particular issue, as well as on the relative power and resources at their disposal. The "unstable" stakeholders are highly prone to shifts in posture, and there is always a danger of them becoming "hostile" stakeholders.

It would be wrong to assume that any one executive could manage all the diverse stakeholders. Stakeholder response strategies should be determined by the entire group and should reflect core values of the organization. Once you have agreed on some generic strategies for dealing with stakeholder dissatisfaction, you can make action plans for when you return to the workplace.

References

Blair, J.D., & Fottler, M.D. (1998). Effective stakeholder management: Challenges, opportunities and strategies. In W.J. Duncan, P.M. Ginter, & L.E. Swayne (Eds.), *Handbook of health care management* (pp. 19–54). Malden, MA: Blackwell.

Ginter, P.M., Swayne, L.E., & Duncan, W.J. (1998). *Strategic management of health care organizations* (3rd ed.) (pp. 39–75). Malden, MA: Blackwell.

"Those Who Matter" Stakeholder Categories

Based on their potential for cooperation and conflict, stakeholders could be broadly categorized into four types, as shown below.

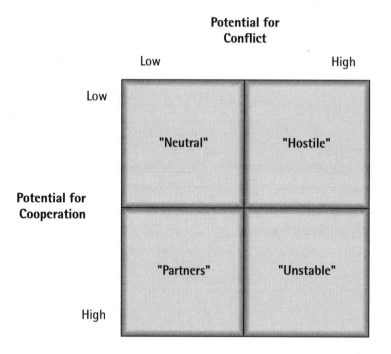

Modified from J.D. Blair and M.D. Fottler (1998). Effective stakeholder management: Challenges, opportunities and strategies. In W.J. Duncan, P.M. Ginter, & L.E. Swayne (Eds.), *Handbook of health care management* (pp. 19–54). Malden, MA: Blackwell.

"Those Who Matter" Individual Worksheet

As we discussed, "stakeholders" are individuals (for example, within a health care organization, patients or physicians), groups (consumer groups, professional associations), or institutions (competitors, media, regulatory agencies) that have significant influence over the way your organization functions and its policies, decisions, and actions. The most powerful among the stakeholders are external to the organization, and you have little or no control over them. Every stakeholder has a unique set of expectations from your organization. Organizational leaders are responsible for handling some powerful stakeholders every day.

Instructions: Working silently, identify and write down those external stakeholders who have significant influence over your organization's decisions and actions. Next, indicate each one's most important expectations from your organization. There could be more than one expectation from each stakeholder. List as many expectations as you can. Also indicate the type of influence the stakeholder has. (An example from the health care industry is given.) Use additional paper, if needed.

External Stakeholder	Expectation(s) of Your Organization	Power to Influence
Outpatient clinics	*Expect higher incentives*	*Expect patient referrals*

External Stakeholder	Expectation(s) of Your Organization	Power to Influence

"Those Who Matter" Generic Strategies for Dealing with Stakeholders

The stakeholders as classified in the following table—a sample from a health care organization—need not necessarily belong in that category forever. As stated earlier, a stakeholder's conflict or cooperation potential depends on its relative power position, relative importance of the issue/problem, and met or unmet expectations. Look at the sample and then fill in your own information.

Stake-holder Type	Stakeholders	Goal of Stakeholder Management	Generic Strategies
Partners	*Board of trustees, senior managers, staff employees, parent organization, local community, referring clinics*	*Maximize their cooperation potential*	*• Encourage participation in the activities of the organization* *• Manage patient relations* *• Involve them in quality management programs* *• Foster a sense of partnership*
Neutral	*Community-based interest groups, professional associations, stockholders*	*Maintain the status quo in stakeholder relationship*	*• Reach out with positive information* *• Keep them informed of organization's activities and services*
Unstable	*Physician consultants, insurance companies, insured patients, complementary non-competing hospitals, referral clinics, special interest groups, patient families*	*Convert them to become "partner" stakeholders or prevent from becoming "hostile" stakeholders*	*• Form mutually beneficial alliances/partnerships/ joint ventures/contractual agreements/mergers* *• Develop referral networks* *• Use aggressive customer relations management* *• Publicize anecdotal evidence of best practices*
Hostile	*Competing hospitals, free-standing specialty clinics, employee unions, regulatory bodies, news media, self-paying patients*	*Defend against negative image and the resultant "costs" thereof*	*• Meet the expectations at the least cost* *• Be proactive in creating social image* *• Deploy better organizational and management systems*

Stake-holder Type	Stakeholders	Goal of Stakeholder Management	Generic Strategies

"Those Who Matter" Group Worksheet

Instructions: List the stakeholders assigned to your subgroup. Note their expectations from your organization. Discuss the likely behavior (or the outcome) for the stakeholder if his or her expectation(s) is not met by your organization. Record the group's observations in single statements. Start from the most adverse or hostile behavior or outcome ("worst case" scenario). Also discuss how the organization might respond to any such adverse or hostile behavior from each stakeholder. While discussing the organization's response strategy, keep in mind the type of influence stakeholders are capable of. Record your group's ideas directly on this sheet.

Stakeholder(s):

Stakeholder Expectation:

Likely behavior or outcome in case of unmet expectation(s)

Response strategy to deal with hostile behavior or adverse outcome

Introduction
to the Editor's Choice Section

The Editor's Choice Section is a collection of contributions that simply do not fit into one of the other three sections: Experiential Learning Activities; Inventories, Questionnaires, and Surveys; and Articles and Discussion Resources. In the past we have had to reject exceptional work that did not meet the criteria of one of the sections or did not fit in one of the categories. The Editor's Choice section allows us to publish these unique items that are useful to the profession, rather than turn them down.

Due to the mere definition of the section, it is difficult to predict what you may find. You may anticipate a potpourri of topics, a variety of formats, and an assortment of categories. Some may be directly related to the training and consulting fields, and others may be related tangentially. Some may be obvious additions and others may not. What you are sure to find is something you may not have expected but that will contribute to your growth and stretch your thinking.

Suffice it to say that this section will provide you with a variety of useful ideas, practical strategies, and creative ways to look at the world. The material will add innovation to your training and consulting knowledge and skills. The contributions will challenge you to think differently, consider a new perspective, and add information you may not have considered before. The contents of this section will stretch your view of training and consulting topics.

The 2004 Pfeiffer Annual: Consulting includes two editor's choice items this year: an activity and an article.

Activity

Four Questions: Managing Change, by Steve Sphar

Intended for newer group leaders, this activity is not, strictly speaking, an experiential learning activity, but we believe it to be a highly useful technique for managing change in organizations.

Article

Building Bench Strength Today for Tomorrow's Success,
by Peter R. Garber and Michael Bergdahl

This article discusses the talent crisis facing many organizations today. Isn't it wise to establish a strategy to attract and retain talent before the crisis hits? The authors explore the steps an organization can take to identify sources of talent from within and outside the organization. Given the gravity of the talent crisis, this article has also been chosen as a cutting-edge topic.

Other materials related to the contributions in the Editor's Choice section can be located in past *Annuals*. You may use our comprehensive *Reference Guide to Handbooks and Annuals* that indexes the contents of all the *Annuals* and the *Handbooks of Structured Experiences*. With each revision, the *Reference Guide* becomes a complete, up-to-date, and easy-to-use resource for selecting appropriate materials from the *Annuals* and *Handbooks*. A print version of the *Reference Guide* is available for volumes through 1999. An online supplement covering the years through 2003 can be found at www.pfeiffer. com/go/supplement.

Due to the nature of the submissions in this section, the pieces encompass a wide range of topics that may not have been indexed in the past. If you do not find what you are looking for under a key word suggested by the article, check related key words. In addition, explore the contents of both volumes of the *Annual*. The division between the two professions, consulting and training, continues to blur. You will find valuable material in both volumes.

Four Questions:
Managing Change

Activity Summary

A quick method for group leaders to manage change in organizations.

Goals

- To give managers a practical tool for managing change with their staff.

- To allow employees input into changes affecting them.

Group Size

Intact work units, up to 30 people per group.

Time Required

Two meetings, from 1 to 2 hours each.

Materials

- A copy of the Four Questions Worksheet for each participant.

- One flip chart with paper.

- Felt-tipped markers.

- Masking tape.

Physical Setting

Tables and chairs arranged so that the participants can hear each other.

Facilitating Risk Taking

Low.

Process

1. Begin this process by meeting with the manager of an intact work unit that is facing an upcoming change. Bring a copy of the Four Questions Worksheet for each person at the meeting. Explain as a brief overview that this is a two-stage process. In the first stage, the manager, with the help of the consultant, answers the first three questions according to his or her best judgment. In the second stage, the manager meets with his or her staff, presents his or her answers, and obtains the staff's answers to the first three questions and the fourth question.

2. To begin stage one, the consultant leads the manager through a discussion of the first question, "What is the change?" in as much detail as possible. The change can be anything—entering a new market, physically relocating a facility, or changing the software platform people are using. Ask the manager to define the change as specifically as possible. While many of these areas may be uncertain at the present time, it is still important to describe as much about the change as is known. It is sufficient to answer the question by stating how much is known at the present and when more information will be available. It is also very important to describe what is NOT changing. During times of change, rumors tend to gain momentum. Describing what is not changing is a way of defining the extent of the change that can reduce anxiety. The following questions can aid this discussion:

   - Does this involve a change to the organizational structure of the unit?

   - Will it result in physical changes, such as new equipment or moving to a new work space?

   - Will the nature of the work done by the unit change?

   - Does this require a change in the number or type of personnel?

   - Will there be new or different roles, job duties, or reporting relationships in the unit?

   - When is the change expected to begin and end?

   (20 minutes.)

3. Once the change has been defined with reasonable specificity, lead the manager through a discussion of the second question, "What are the reasons for/ benefits of the change?" Probe for benefits to staff, such as a chance to learn new skills, a more profitable product line, easier or faster access to information, or more challenging work. Have the manager describe the benefits in some detail. However, some changes, such as layoffs, do not have immediate or tangible benefits to staff. It is still important to identify the problem or issue that led to the change and to explain how this change is expected to remedy the situation.
    (20 minutes.)

4. Ask the manager to consider the third question, "How will the change affect the individuals who experience it?" Have him or her describe how people will be affected. Questions that can aid this discussion include:

    - Are staffing changes being made?

    - Will assignments, schedules, or job duties change?

    - Will staff need new skills?

    - Will staff receive adequate training?

    - What losses will people experience from the change?

    (20 minutes.)

5. The manager is now ready for stage two. Ask the manager to call a meeting with his or her staff. Distribute copies of the "Four Questions Worksheet" and pencils to the staff members. Have the manager give and explain his or her answers to the first question, "What is the change?" while the group takes notes. Ask for questions, comments, or input from the group. If necessary, the consultant can record important points on the flip chart. If the change is seen differently by staff from what was expressed by the manager, point out the differences and ask for clarification.
    (15 minutes.)

6. When the group is through discussing question one, ask the manager to give his or her answer to question two, "What are the reasons for/benefits of the change?" Again, ask for questions, comments, or input from the group. Record important points on the flip chart. Staff may have very different perceptions of the reasons for or benefits of the change. It is not important that staff agree completely with the manager. There is considerable benefit to be gained from allowing staff to express their views and to be heard. This discussion can also lead to new information and insights for the manager.
    (15 minutes.)

7. Have the manager now present answers to the third question, "How will the change affect the individuals who experience it?" Ask for questions, comments, or input from the group. If staff see additional ways that the change affects them, list these on the flip chart.
(15 minutes.)

8. Summarize the basic points of the discussion and ask the group to provide answers to the fourth question, "What supports and tools will people need to manage the transition?" If the group is small (5 to 8) or if the participants feel comfortable speaking in the large group, have them brainstorm and record their answers on a flip chart. If the group is large (10 or more) or if some members seem hesitant to speak up, the group can be divided into pairs or trios.
(15 minutes.)

9. End the session by pointing out the benefits from having held the discussion:

- All have heard each other's views and concerns about the impending change.

- All have learned new information about the change.

- They have produced a list of tools and supports that can help the group navigate the change.
(15 minutes.)

10. Encourage everyone to make action plans for dealing with the change when they return to the job, especially addressing the manager's role in providing needed tools and support systems. Ask for closing comments from each person in turn.
(10 minutes.)

Submitted by Steve Sphar.

Steve Sphar, J.D., *is an internal organization development consultant for the California State Teachers' Retirement System. He has counseled managers and employees in both the private and public sectors for over fifteen years. He is a frequent contributor to professional publications, including the* Annuals *and the McGraw-Hill* Training and Performance Sourcebook.

Four Questions Worksheet

1. What is the change?

2. What are the reasons for/benefits of the change?

3. How will the change affect the individuals who experience it?

4. What supports and tools will people need to manage the transition?

Building Bench Strength Today for Tomorrow's Success

Peter R. Garber and Michael Bergdahl

Summary

Organizations are totally dependent on the talent of their employees to achieve both current and desired goals for success. Talent separates good organizations from great organizations. Obviously, those companies that are most successful in attracting and retaining the most talented employees will outperform their competition. From this talent pool the highest caliber leaders are found. The tremendous influence that extraordinary leadership can have on an organization is evidenced by the successes of such companies as General Electric and Wal-Mart. Every company must have an effective strategy in place to continuously bring in and retain the best talent in order to remain competitive in the future. But a talent crisis exists today that will intensify in the future for organizations of all types and sizes.

The Talent Crisis

In terms of talent acquisition, the future has already arrived. You need to begin your bench-building process today to fill tomorrow's talent needs. Too often, organizations delay this process until they find themselves in a succession crisis. Traditional succession planning processes too often are not used until there is an opening. Then the mad scramble begins, as the organization has to scour its ranks for someone who can fit into the now urgent vacancy that exists or search in desperation for a replacement on the open market. Rather than continuing to repeat this harrowing experience every time your organization experiences attrition (either expected or unexpected), you must build and manage a succession pool of candidates for projected openings in the future.

Talent Search

You don't have to be the host of the popular television program "Star Search"—introducing the next aspiring performer and hopeful superstar of tomorrow—but you do need a process to identify talent inside your organization. Not everyone can be a star in your organization. (Actually, it wouldn't be a desirable situation to have nothing but stars working for you.) You must have supporting players with a diversity of talent to keep things running effectively and efficiently fulfilling a variety of needs at different levels of performance. But all organizations want and need star performers as well, as they often make the biggest difference in the ultimate success of the business. Identifying and acquiring this level of talent is often a really big challenge.

Typically, the costs associated with acquiring the talent an organization anticipates it may need in the future causes the process to be postponed, or even abandoned. This is particularly true during hard economic times. This may be understandable if (1) the need is not immediate, (2) there is not a current crisis to be addressed, and (3) the investment has a delayed return. However, down times are the most important time to be searching for talent. You may be able to find the best candidates at the most reasonable costs. If you wait until better economic times, the same level of talent may not be available or, if it is, it may only be available at a premium price.

Too often, organizations look for talent in all the wrong places. You get what you give. Talent begets talent: talented people want to work with other talented people. Take advantage of the talent you have to find other talented people. It's like playing a matchmaker role. Fish in the talent pool. Like any good fisherman, find the best spots to drop your line, ones that haven't already been fished out by the competition.

Find new talent sources and tap into different talent networks. You may not know when you have caught the best talent or recognize that high-potential candidate when he or she walks in. Dive in headfirst and arranging that "blind date" between a candidate and your company. The best thing may be to rely on your instincts rather than overanalyzing the situation.

Organizational Learning from the Outside In

Organizations learn and develop in many ways. This learning process can be greatly accelerated by the talent that exists in the organization. Talented employees create many advantages for the organization. For example, the more talented your employees, the greater the advantage you will have over your competition.

Any *talent infusion* can have a significant impact on your organization. However, it can also shock the system if not managed properly, resulting in *talent dilution*. Think about bringing in an infusion of talent. How will acquired talent change the corporate culture? Will it create a talent identity crisis and cause dissatisfaction among the talented people already working for you?

These are legitimate questions as you begin to think about acquiring talent. Perhaps the first question is whether the same talent exists within your organization. Finding out may turn out to be more a strategic than an immediate objective, but something to explore.

Your goal should always be to attract, retain, and upgrade the talent in your organization. Identify the attributes that your organization needs to be successful in the future. Create a talent competency model that describes precisely what these attributes are and how they can be acquired. Based on this model, provide the necessary opportunities for your employees to acquire or develop these attributes through training, mentoring, developmental assignments, or management development.

Talent Strategies

Many organizations do not have an effective strategy or plan in place to guide the process. Their initiatives are sporadic and hurried and seldom address the potential problems that acquiring new talent can create internally.

You must have a vision of what you want in your organization. Begin by introducing "bench building" into your culture. "Calendarize" bench building; do it each year regardless of outside influences. Create a bench strength matrix to rank the potential of current employees to help you visualize where you are strongest as well as weakest.

An example of a *bench strength matrix* is shown in Exhibit 1. This matrix shows the strongest possibilities for replacing a corporate communications manager in the future and where the organization may need to do some recruiting or development to improve its bench strength for this position.

Corporate Communications Manager	Readiness for the Position 1 to 5 (highest)
Joe Smith	5
Sally Green	4
Dan Rodgers	3
Kelly Kline	3
Henry Bates	1

Exhibit 1. Bench Strength Matrix

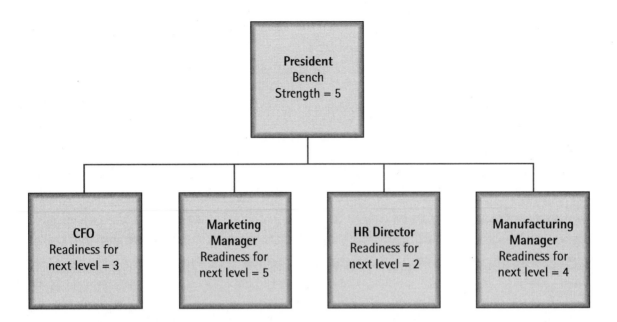

Exhibit 2. Succession Planning Organization Chart

You can also create a *succession planning organization chart* to visualize the greatest bench-building weaknesses as well as strengths. In the chart in Exhibit 2, each potential successor for the position of president is rated for his or her readiness (with 1 being least ready and 5 most ready).

By using these tools, you can create strategies for improving staffing in the future. Set goals for capture rates for the talent you wish to acquire and identify where you need to seed talent in the organization.

Talent Lifecycles

Like any dynamic process, talent goes in cycles. Understanding these cycles is critical to planning, acquiring, and nurturing talent effectively. For example, there is a certain time in any employee's career—usually in the later stages—when his or her talent potential is at its highest. Knowing where employees are in this cycle is a critical part of your overall talent strategy. If there is not a diversity of years of service and experience in your organization, you could be headed for a talent crisis. Strive to have a healthy balance of experience levels in your organization at all times.

An unfortunate reality is *talent attrition*. Attrition can occur for a number of reasons, some controllable, some not. Longer attrition cycles can positively influence talent lifecycles. Therefore, you have to have an *attrition plan* as well as a talent acquisition plan. Part of your overall talent strategy should be determining the mix of lifers (employees who spend their entire careers with the organization) with acquired talent. The ideal ratio will be dependent on your organization's needs, both immediate and future. You don't want either group dominating the other. An ideal ratio might be 50/50 so each viewpoint is adequately represented. Identifying the ideal balance will help you determine your targeted attrition rate. Identifying career paths that are in alignment with the goals and expectations of the talent you wish to retain or acquire is critically important.

Opportunistic hiring, that is, creating or finding positions for talented candidates as they become available, rather than making hiring decisions based entirely on current or anticipated needs, can be an important component of any talent acquisition strategy. But acquiring top talent is only part of the challenge. You must also motivate talented individuals so they are not wooed away by another organization with the same objectives as yours.

Institutionalizing Talent

The talent acquisition process must be *institutionalized* in order to preserve it in the future. Organizations must realize that they are only as good as the talent that exists within their grasp, both internally and externally. Top management must support and sponsor talent initiatives, both in acquisition and retention. They must view talent the same as any other asset. Attention, effort, and money must by expended in order to capitalize on and realize the intended return on any investment, including talent. Talent should not be viewed as something that would be *nice* to have, but as something that is *essential* to your organization's future.

Diversity in Talent Initiatives

A potential obstacle to successful talent acquisition is the perpetuation of the same organizational personality and culture that has always existed. There may be nothing wrong with it at this point but, if left unchallenged and unchanging, it may not serve the organization well in the future.

Organizations have personalities much the same as people do, and these are typically reflective of the diversity of the talent within the organization. To thrive, organizations must continually bring in new ideas and philosophies that reflect the world in which they operate. There is no better portal for this diversity than talent acquisition. There is perhaps no better way to break an existing corporate mold than diversifying your talent pool.

Talent today is much different from in the past. Talent acquisition is perhaps your best opportunity to increase the odds of your organization surviving in the future.

Peter R. Garber *is manager of affirmative action for PPG Industries Inc., in Pittsburgh, Pennsylvania. He is the author of five management books, including his most recent work,* Turbulent Change: Every Working Person's Survival Guide, *and is a regular contributor of activities and learning instruments to the* Annuals.

Michael Bergdahl *is a graduate of Penn State University and has held human resource positions at Frito-Lay, Wal-Mart, American Eagle, and Waste Management. He is currently a keynote speaker, writer, and business consultant based in Pittsburgh, Pennsylvania.*

Introduction
to the Inventories, Questionnaires, and Surveys Section

Inventories, questionnaires, and surveys are valuable tools for the HRD professional. These feedback tools help respondents take an objective look at themselves and at their organizations. These tools also help to explain how a particular theory applies to them or to their situations.

Inventories, questionnaires, and surveys are useful in a number of training and consulting situations: privately for self-diagnosis; one-on-one to plan individual development; in a small group to open discussion; in a work team to help the team to focus on its highest priorities; or in an organization to gather data to achieve progress.

You will find that the use of inventories, questionnaires, and surveys enriches, personalizes, and deepens training, development, and intervention designs. Many can be combined with experiential learning activities or articles in this or other *Annuals* to design an exciting, involving, practical, and well-rounded intervention.

Each instrument includes the background necessary for understanding, presenting, and using it. Interpretive information, scales, and scoring sheets are also provided. In addition, we include the reliability and validity data contributed by the authors. If you wish additional information on any of these instruments, contact the authors directly. You will find their addresses and telephone numbers in the "Contributors" listing near the end of this volume.

Other assessment tools that address a wider variety of topics can be found in our comprehensive *Reference Guide to Handbooks and Annuals*. This guide indexes all the instruments that we have published to date in the *Annuals*. You will find this complete, up-to-date, and easy-to-use resource valuable for locating other instruments, as well as for locating experiential learning activities and articles. A print version of the *Reference Guide* is available for volumes through 1999. An online supplement covering the years through 2003 can be found at www.pfeiffer.com/go/supplement.

The 2004 Pfeiffer Annual: Consulting includes three assessment tools in the following categories:

Individual Development

Simulations: Pre- and Post-Evaluations of Performance, by Ira J. Morrow

Leadership

Organizational Frames Analysis: A Tool to Enhance Leadership, by John Sample and Martha C. Yopp

Organizations

The Web-Based Learning Readiness Inventory (WLRI): Is Your Organization Ready for the Information Superhighway? by Douglas J. Swiatkowski and Amy Pawlusiak

Simulations: Pre- and Post-Evaluations of Performance

Ira J. Morrow

Summary

Large-scale behavioral simulations are frequently used in management education and in training and development programs. However, these simulations generally do not include a way to provide quantitative or qualitative feedback to participants, thus limiting the potential for learning from them. The three evaluation instruments presented here are a way for participants to receive feedback from peers and to do self-assessment immediately before and after a simulation. Ways to use these instruments to help participants reflect on their performance, learn how they are perceived by others, develop insight about themselves, and obtain the information needed to improve their managerial performance are discussed.

Ever since the development of "Looking Glass" by the Center for Creative Leadership in Greensboro, North Carolina, in 1983, the use of large-scale behavioral simulations to enhance the realism and value of management training, development, and education programs has become common. Such simulations provide the means for introducing participants to the complexity and ambiguity of organizational life and decision making and to the value of teamwork, cooperation, coordination, and communication. Opportunities are generally provided for experimenting with new behaviors and for demonstrating and enhancing leadership skills, the ability to influence others, and problem-solving skills, all of which are critically important in today's business world.

Experience with various large-scale behavioral simulations suggests that their potential value is enhanced not only by a comprehensive debriefing session led by an experienced facilitator, but by providing participants with opportunities to evaluate the effectiveness of their own performance and the performance of their peers during the simulation. Such feedback allows participants to more fully capitalize on the learning potential of the simulation and provides the basis for subsequent efforts to alter or improve performance. It is in this regard, however, that most large-scale behavioral simulations are lacking. That is, the materials that are supplied to users generally do not include adequate feedback mechanisms.

The three instruments presented here provide a way to obtain self and peer feedback. Suggestions for discussion of the results are provided that will result in self-reflection and greater insight on one's own behavior.

These instruments are not designed to be used with any particular large-scale behavioral simulation product, but can be adapted for use with any simulation package used for management development.

Description of the Instruments

Pre-Simulation Self-Assessment (Instrument 1)

The Pre-Simulation Self-Assessment consists of twenty-nine items with a five-point response scale ranging from 1 (very dissatisfied) to 5 (very satisfied). One item asks participants how satisfied they think they will be with their overall performance, and another asks them to predict their satisfaction with others' overall performance. Specific behavioral dimensions related to effectiveness as a manager are addressed, including goal setting, time management, stress management, ability to delegate, decision making, problem solving, creativity, motivation, the ability to motivate others, sensitivity to others, listening, assertiveness, diplomacy, ability to win others' trust and to trust others, self-disclosure, negotiation, team contribution, conflict management, consensus building, ability to change, communication, influencing, leadership, use of power, energy level, and ability to work hard. The instrument concludes with three open-ended items that ask participants which of their skills they believe will help them the most, which they are most concerned about needing during the simulation, and how they think their performance is likely to change over time.

Theory Behind Instrument 1

The twenty-nine items reflect issues that frequently come up in management and leadership training and development programs due to their relationship to managerial performance. Not surprisingly, such issues are usually embedded within large-scale behavioral simulations and may be emphasized by particular consultants and trainers. Moreover, as one would expect, such issues are frequently discussed in skills-oriented management books, such as Whetten and Cameron (2002).

Administration of Instrument 1

It is suggested that a general description of the simulation and its training or developmental objectives be given, as well as a brief overview of the simulated company/situation and its structure/tasks. Generally in a simulation, an annual report describing the history, structure, and performance of the company is distributed to participants, and they are likely to receive an organizational chart as well. In most such simulations, participants are assigned to fill specific positions. This can be done in several ways, including self-nomination, assignment through discussion and consensus agreement by teams or groups, or appointment by the facilitator. Prior to receiving in-baskets of written memoranda, letters, and reports custom-designed for their assigned positions, all participants may receive a pre-work package of general information, memos, and reports about the company. In any case, at some point during this introduction, orientation, and familiarization process, participants will develop increasingly informed impressions of what the simulation is about and the demands it might make on them. They will also start to feel how well they are likely to perform during the simulation. These feelings will range from the extremely pessimistic to the extremely optimistic. The Pre-Simulation Evaluation gives respondents an outlet for their feelings and perceptions along specific behavioral and skill dimensions.

This instrument should be completed by participants after they have received their general orientation to the program, been assigned to teams, seen an organizational chart, and been appointed to or have selected a specific position, but before receiving their individualized in-baskets of materials. Participants should be told in advance whether this instrument and subsequent assessment instruments will be collected and seen by the instructor, facilitator, or assigned observers or whether only they will see and keep the completed instrument. In any case, the advantages of frank and honest self-reporting on all assessment instruments should be stressed. Encourage as much honesty as possible by giving complete control, use of, and access to assessment instruments to the participants themselves. You may choose to collect the instruments, and certainly a case can be made for this approach as well. One factor that should weigh in the decision of "to collect or not to collect" is whether the simulation is being used primarily for individual or team skill development or for assessment. Familiarize respondents with the instrument by walking them through it. The Pre-Simulation Self-Assessment instrument should take approximately 10 or 15 minutes to complete.

The Scoring Process for Instrument 1

The scoring of this instrument is direct in that the score for each rating item is simply what was given by the respondent without any conversion of the scores. A total score and an average score can be calculated for the twenty-nine rated items.

Further ways to use the scores on this instrument are discussed in conjunction with scoring of the Post-Simulation Evaluation instrument below.

Post-Simulation Evaluation (Instrument 2)

The Post-Simulation Evaluation includes the same twenty-nine items and five-point response scale used for the Pre-Simulation Evaluation (Instrument 1) described above. The intention is to allow for the comparison of pre- and post-scores on an item-by-item basis. The major distinction between the two instruments is that, whereas the Pre-Simulation Self-Assessment asks participants, "Based on what you have heard about this simulation, how satisfied do you think you will be with the following," the Post-Simulation Evaluation asks, "Based on what you have experienced during this simulation, how satisfied are you with the following." Another distinction between the two instruments is in the open-ended questions section, which is more comprehensive and probing for the Post-Simulation Evaluation, as participants now know their behaviors and performance. The open-ended questions for Instrument 2 ask participants about the skills that helped them the most while working through the simulation and which skills, if improved, would enhance their performance. Other areas addressed include how their behavior changed over time during the simulation, their views on who contributed the most to the effectiveness of their team and how, lessons they learned from observing others during the simulation, and how they would rank themselves compared to the way they feel that others would rank them in terms of their overall contribution to the team. In addition, participants are asked to comment on who they helped the most and who helped them the most during the simulation, which simulation event or achievement they are most proud of, and what they would do differently if they could repeat the simulation. Finally, participants are given an opportunity to reflect on what they learned about themselves and about management and leadership from the simulation.

Theory Behind Instrument 2

Since the twenty-nine rated items are the same here as for the first instrument, the same logic and theoretical rationale for their use applies. The issue that is likely to come up when using this instrument is the theoretical rationale for having respondents rate the same items again. Simply highlight the difference between forming expectations of one's performance based on performance in similar experiences or on rumors, hearsay, and emotions, on the one hand, and looking back and reflecting in a more informed manner on one's performance after the performance has taken place. The theoretical rationale for gathering data pre-simulation and post-simulation is similar to the rationale for action research, where there is a pre-measurement, an intervention, and then post-measurement.

Here, however, the participant's skills may have been enhanced from pre- to post-measurement by participating in the simulation, which is the rationale for its use as a training and development tool. Thus, you are providing the measurement tools to compare how participants feel they will perform before the simulation begins and how they think that they did perform now that the simulation has ended. This in turn relates to how we form expectations, the accuracy of our expectations, and our self-insight, issues that are discussed further below.

Administration of Instrument 2

At the conclusion of the interactive phase of a large-scale behavioral simulation, a number of closing activities are likely to take place. Often, some participants, including but not limited to the participant who holds the most senior position in the simulation, are asked to prepare a presentation to the rest of the simulated company (the other participants) about the state of the organization. Generally, all simulation-related activities following these presentations are designed to help debrief participants, to provide opportunities for venting, and to discuss the events of the simulation and the simulated organization's performance. In addition, it is useful to allow participants to reflect in a more formalized and structured fashion on how they feel they performed as individuals. Instrument 2 is designed for this purpose.

Facilitators should walk participants through the instrument, point out similarities to and differences from the Pre-Simulation Self-Assessment, encourage frank and honest responses, and discuss who—if anyone besides the respondent—will see this information. Completion of this instrument should take approximately 15 to 20 minutes.

Scoring Process for Instruments 1 and 2

Actively encourage participants to take the time and effort needed to make comparisons between their pre- and post-scores. They can calculate an overall summary and an average score for the entire set of items and compare these figures. They can also examine scores on an item-by-item basis for the purpose of identifying particular skill areas where their scores increased, decreased, or remained the same.

Encourage respondents to look for patterns that emerge in particular areas or skill domains in which their self-perceptions improved or deteriorated and to try to account for the specific events or behaviors in the simulation that may explain differences in scores. This could logically lead to a discussion of the importance of self-knowledge, self-insight, and of having a realistic self-image.

Stress the importance of individuals becoming more knowledgeable about how they confront and deal with different situations, including those that are intentionally complex and ambiguous. Discuss how their expectations should increasingly become more in line with actual outcomes.

Post-Simulation Peer Assessment (Instrument 3)

The Post-Simulation Peer Assessment contains an open-ended section that asks for a listing of effective and ineffective behaviors observed, suggested developmental needs, and specific developmental recommendations or actions to be taken. It also includes twenty-eight items with the same five-point rating scale used in the prior two instruments. The stem statement for these items reads: "Based on what I observed of your behavior in the simulation, I would rate your performance as follows." These items correspond to the items and skill areas measured in the previous instruments, with the exception of one item. The last section of the instrument contains four additional open-ended questions asking respondents to indicate the skills that helped the participant being rated the most during the simulation, how the participant's behavior changed over time, when the participant was at his or her best, and which other participant the participant being rated helped the most.

Theory Behind Instrument 3

One of the most important and beneficial aspects of the use of large-scale behavioral simulations is their emphasis on social interaction and working with others. Clearly, in light of the duration and intensity of these experiences, participants generally have extensive opportunities to form perceptions of others and how they perform.

Besides providing participants with a structured format for reflecting on their own performance, it can be equally or more rewarding to provide a structured and formalized means for receiving both quantitative and qualitative feedback from peers. The importance of feedback from others about one's own performance is of course widely recognized in the management literature (Luthans, 1998; Whetten & Cameron, 2002). Aside from simply allowing participants to receive quantitative behavioral feedback from others, a relatively rare and valuable event in and of itself, the Post-Simulation Peer Assessment enables participants to compare their self-perceptions with the perceptions of others. The importance of this process is emphasized by Haney (1992), who states: "The handicap of inaccurate self-knowledge and the unwillingness to construct a more realistic self-image seem to be very widespread. In thirty-five years of organizational research and consulting, I have known scores if not hundreds . . . who seemed to have all the requisites for continued success . . . but they had one vital failing—they did not know themselves. The image they held of themselves was pitifully out of phase with that which they were projecting to others. To successfully discharge the responsibilities of a challenging, people-oriented position requires the possession of a more-than-ordinarily-realistic self-image—an exceptionally realistic self-image."

Thus, all three of the instruments provided here may be thought of as tools for enabling participants in large-scale behavioral simulations to develop a more realistic self-image.

Administration of Instrument 3

This instrument is designed to be given to a particular participant, but it is completed anonymously to encourage frank feedback. Working with the organizational chart, the facilitator may provide general guidance as to which individuals should be providing feedback to whom. The facilitator can also gather the completed forms solely for the purpose of sorting them by recipient for subsequent delivery to that person. The facilitator can keep track of who has not received adequate feedback in order to encourage those who worked with that person to give it. Depending on the number of participants in the simulation, the facilitator can indicate a minimum number of peer feedback forms that each individual should receive. Obviously, the more feedback the better, but since time is always a constraint, a minimum of three forms for each participant is a good target.

Interpreting Scores for Instrument 3

There is an obvious value in providing participants with written quantitative and qualitative feedback from peers whom they worked closely with during the simulation. It gives participants something concrete to leave the simulation with, to file away, and to refer back to on occasion as a way to check their progress in developing or enhancing their management skills and performance in the future.

It should be stressed to participants that the feedback they have received reflects the way they are perceived by others—specific to their actions during the simulation. Perceptions do not constitute reality, and in fact, in complex organizations reality is often ambiguous, not totally known, and largely socially constructed. However, for better or worse, perceptions do matter, and they can determine our career success or failure. Advise participants to look for patterns that emerge as they digest the peer feedback they have received and to give less weight to discrepant or idiosyncratic feedback and more to convergent or consistent feedback.

Other Suggested Uses for Instruments 2 and 3

A less obvious, but potentially striking use of the Post-Simulation Peer Assessment is to provide the additional data needed to make comparisons between peer post-simulation ratings and the self post-simulation ratings. Average scores for all the peer item ratings can be calculated and compared to the average for all the self item ratings. Peer feedback item-by-item average scores can be calculated as well and compared to individual item scores. When there is close agreement between self and average peer ratings in an area, that is, when one's self-perception is consistent with the way others perceive one, it suggests the presence of a more realistic self-image.

However, to the extent that one's self-ratings were inconsistent with peer feedback, one's self-image as to performance in the simulation was not in line with reality. In this case, questions of accuracy are largely irrelevant, since reality is socially constructed. Unfortunately, although others' perceptions may be off the mark, they nevertheless matter. More important questions to consider are the direction of the discrepancy. The pattern of overly inflated self-ratings and less flattering peer ratings suggests that either a person is overestimating his or her performance in terms of its impact on others or that, for some reason, his or her potential strengths are not being picked up on by others. The question then is whether this is a pattern that emerges in other settings as well. If this is the case, there may be value in learning to adjust one's self-image to be more consistent with the views of others or in changing one's performance so that one's self-perceived strengths become more obvious to others. When the pattern is one of weak self-ratings, but more glowing peer ratings, the participant may be underestimating his or her performance in terms of its impact on others and may be prone to self-doubt. The question in this case is whether or not this is a pattern that emerges in other settings as well and what the reasons and implications for the future might be. There could well be an argument in favor of learning to adjust one's self-image upward to be more in step with the perceptions of others.

Summary

In summary, the three assessment instruments described here may be used in conjunction with large-scale behavioral simulations that are frequently found in management development programs. Instrument scores can be retained for long-term analysis and reflection by participants, providing the information that participants may need to capitalize fully on the great learning potential inherent in the use of simulations, to develop a more realistic self-image, or to modify skills and behavior in order to be more effective in the managerial roles and assignments that await them in the future.

Reliability and Validity of the Instruments

The three instruments discussed here are designed to stimulate personal reflection on one's skills and performance as exhibited in a single developmental episode, namely in a large-scale behavioral simulation. They are not meant to measure more enduring or general qualities possessed by the person or exhibited in other settings. As such they constitute a training and development tool that may be used in conjunction with large-scale simulations.

The items have face validity in that they address the management and leadership skill issues discussed in the literature and generally embedded in such simulations. There is no implication that any of these instruments measures a single construct, so neither inter-item reliability nor construct validity pertain. In fact, a strong case can be made that scores should differ widely on different items in that they refer to different skills. Test-retest reliability is also not relevant in this case, in that we would expect scores to change with each participation in a different simulation and with interactions with different sets of peers in these simulations.

References

Haney, W.V. (1992). *Communication and interpersonal relations* (6th ed.). Homewood, IL: Richard D. Irwin.

Luthans, F. (1998). *Organizational behavior* (8th ed.). New York: McGraw-Hill.

Whetten, D.A., & Cameron, K.S. (2002). *Developing management skills* (5th ed.). Upper Saddle River, NJ: Prentice Hall.

Ira J. Morrow *has a Ph.D. degree in industrial-organizational psychology from New York University, and he is currently associate professor of management at Pace University. He works with M.B.A. students from around the world and is part of a faculty team that designed and implemented a two-semester, skills- and theory-oriented graduate management course at his institution. He consults extensively in the field of human resources with an emphasis on management assessment.*

Pre-Simulation Self-Assessment (Instrument 1)

Ira J. Morrow

Instructions: Based on what you have heard about the simulation we are about to do, predict the level of satisfaction you will have later with the behavior you will exhibit during the simulation, using the following scale:

1 = Very Dissatisfied   4 = Somewhat Satisfied
2 = Somewhat Dissatisfied   5 = Very Satisfied
3 = Neither Satisfied nor Dissatisfied

1a.	How satisfied do you think you will be with *your* overall performance?	1	2	3	4	5
2a.	How satisfied do you think you will be with *others'* overall performance?	1	2	3	4	5

How satisfied do you think you will be with each of the following:

3a.	Your ability to set clear, realistic, demanding goals.	1	2	3	4	5
4a.	Your ability to manage your time effectively.	1	2	3	4	5
5a.	Your ability to handle stress.	1	2	3	4	5
6a.	Your ability to delegate work to others.	1	2	3	4	5
7a.	Your ability to make effective decisions.	1	2	3	4	5
8a.	Your ability to solve problems.	1	2	3	4	5
9a.	Your ability to think of creative ideas.	1	2	3	4	5
10a.	Your own level of motivation.	1	2	3	4	5
11a.	Your ability to motivate others.	1	2	3	4	5
12a.	Your ability to interact with others in a sensitive manner.	1	2	3	4	5
13a.	Your ability to listen to others.	1	2	3	4	5
14a.	Your ability to be assertive.	1	2	3	4	5

1 = Very Dissatisfied	4 = Somewhat Satisfied	
2 = Somewhat Dissatisfied	5 = Very Satisfied	
3 = Neither Satisfied nor Dissatisfied		

15a.	Your ability to treat others in a diplomatic manner.	1 2 3 4 5
16a.	Your ability to gain the trust of others.	1 2 3 4 5
17a.	Your willingness to trust others.	1 2 3 4 5
18a.	Your willingness to disclose information about yourself to others.	1 2 3 4 5
19a.	Your ability to negotiate effectively.	1 2 3 4 5
20a.	Your ability to contribute to the team.	1 2 3 4 5
21a.	Your ability to manage conflict.	1 2 3 4 5
22a.	Your ability to build a consensus.	1 2 3 4 5
23a.	Your willingness to change when necessary.	1 2 3 4 5
24a.	Your ability to communicate with others.	1 2 3 4 5
25a.	Your ability to persuade/influence others.	1 2 3 4 5
26a.	Your ability to lead others.	1 2 3 4 5
27a.	Your ability to use power effectively.	1 2 3 4 5
28a.	Your energy level.	1 2 3 4 5
29a.	Your ability to work hard.	1 2 3 4 5

Now add up the scores you gave yourself and put the total here: _____

Next average your scores by dividing the total by 29.
Put your average score, carried to two decimal places, here: _____

Open-Ended Questions

- Which of your skills or abilities do you think will help you the most during this simulation? Why?

- Which of your skills or abilities are you most concerned about in this simulation? Why?

- As the simulation takes place, what changes in your behavior are likely to be exhibited over time? Why do you think this?

Notes/Comments:

Post–Simulation Evaluation (Instrument 2)

Ira J. Morrow

Instructions: Based on what you experienced while participating in this simulation, rate your level of satisfaction with your performance by answering the following questions. Circle the appropriate answers based on the following scale:

1 = Very Dissatisfied	**4 = Somewhat Satisfied**
2 = Somewhat Dissatisfied	**5 = Very Satisfied**
3 = Neither Satisfied nor Dissatisfied	

1b.	How satisfied were you with *your* overall performance?	1	2	3	4	5
2b.	How satisfied were you with *others'* overall performance?	1	2	3	4	5

How satisfied were you with the following:

3b.	Your ability to set clear, realistic, demanding goals.	1	2	3	4	5
4b.	Your ability to manage your time effectively.	1	2	3	4	5
5b.	Your ability to handle stress.	1	2	3	4	5
6b.	Your ability to delegate work to others.	1	2	3	4	5
7b.	Your ability to make effective decisions.	1	2	3	4	5
8b.	Your ability to solve problems.	1	2	3	4	5
9b.	Your ability to think of creative ideas.	1	2	3	4	5
10b.	Your own level of motivation.	1	2	3	4	5
11b.	Your ability to motivate others.	1	2	3	4	5
12b.	Your ability to interact with others in a sensitive manner.	1	2	3	4	5
13b.	Your ability to listen to others.	1	2	3	4	5
14b.	Your ability to be assertive.	1	2	3	4	5

1 = Very Dissatisfied	4 = Somewhat Satisfied
2 = Somewhat Dissatisfied	5 = Very Satisfied
3 = Neither Satisfied nor Dissatisfied	

15b.	Your ability to treat others in a diplomatic manner.	1	2	3	4	5
16b.	Your ability to gain the trust of others.	1	2	3	4	5
17b.	Your willingness to trust others.	1	2	3	4	5
18b.	Your willingness to disclose information about yourself to others.	1	2	3	4	5
19b.	Your ability to negotiate effectively.	1	2	3	4	5
20b.	Your ability to contribute to the team.	1	2	3	4	5
21b.	Your ability to manage conflict.	1	2	3	4	5
22b.	Your ability to build a consensus.	1	2	3	4	5
23b.	Your willingness to change when necessary.	1	2	3	4	5
24b.	Your ability to communicate with others.	1	2	3	4	5
25b.	Your ability to persuade/influence others.	1	2	3	4	5
26b.	Your ability to lead others.	1	2	3	4	5
27b.	Your ability to use power effectively.	1	2	3	4	5
28b.	Your energy level.	1	2	3	4	5
29b.	Your ability to work hard.	1	2	3	4	5

Add your selections together to arrive at a total and write it here: _____

Obtain an average score by dividing the total score above by 29 and carrying it to two decimal places. Write the answer here: _____

Open-Ended Questions

- Which of your skills or abilities do you think helped you the most during this simulation? Why?

- Which of your skills or abilities do you particularly have to improve in order to enhance your performance in a simulation of this sort? Why?

- As the simulation took place, what changes in your behavior did you exhibit over time? Why?

- What observations can you make about the performance of others in general?

- In your opinion, which individuals contributed the most to the effectiveness of the team? In what ways did they contribute?

- What lessons did you learn from observing others' behavior during this simulation?

- Where would you rank yourself in terms of your overall contribution to your team? Place an X in the Self-Ranking column below to indicate your belief.

- How do you think your team members would rank you? Place an X in the Peer Ranking column below to indicate your estimate.

	Self-Ranking	Peer Ranking
Top 10 percent		
Top quartile		
Top half		
Bottom half		
Bottom 10 percent		

Explain Your Rankings

- Which people helped you the most? In what ways did they help?

- Which people did you help the most? In what ways did you help?

- What achievement or event are you proudest of when you look back at your performance in this simulation? Why?

- What would you do differently, if you could? Why?

- What did you learn about yourself from this simulation?

- What did you learn about management from this simulation?

Notes/Comments:

Post-Simulation Peer Assessment (Instrument 3)

Ira J. Morrow

Instructions: Write the name of the person you are providing feedback for below.

To: _____

Effective Behaviors I Observed

1.

2.

3.

4.

5.

Ineffective Behaviors I Observed

1.

2.

3.

4.

Developmental Needs I Saw

1.

2.

3.

4.

Developmental Recommendations/Actions

1.

2.

3.

4.

Based on what I observed of your behavior during the simulation, I had the following reactions to your performance:

1 = Very Dissatisfied   **4 = Somewhat Satisfied**
2 = Somewhat Dissatisfied   **5 = Very Satisfied**
3 = Neither Satisfied nor Dissatisfied

1c.	Your overall performance.	1	2	3	4	5
2c.	Your ability to set clear, realistic, demanding goals.	1	2	3	4	5
3c.	Your ability to manage your time effectively.	1	2	3	4	5
4c.	Your ability to handle stress.	1	2	3	4	5
5c.	Your ability to delegate work to others.	1	2	3	4	5
6c.	Your ability to make effective decisions.	1	2	3	4	5
7c.	Your ability to solve problems.	1	2	3	4	5
8c.	Your ability to think of creative ideas.	1	2	3	4	5
9c.	Your own level of motivation.	1	2	3	4	5
10c.	Your ability to motivate others.	1	2	3	4	5
11c.	Your ability to interact with others in a sensitive manner.	1	2	3	4	5
12c.	Your ability to listen to others.	1	2	3	4	5
13c.	Your ability to be assertive.	1	2	3	4	5
14c.	Your ability to treat others in a diplomatic manner.	1	2	3	4	5
15c.	Your ability to gain the trust of others.	1	2	3	4	5
16c.	Your willingness to trust others.	1	2	3	4	5
17c.	Your willingness to disclose information about yourself to others.	1	2	3	4	5
18c.	Your ability to negotiate effectively.	1	2	3	4	5
19c.	Your ability to contribute to the team.	1	2	3	4	5

1 = Very Dissatisfied		**4 = Somewhat Satisfied**	
2 = Somewhat Dissatisfied		**5 = Very Satisfied**	
3 = Neither Satisfied nor Dissatisfied			

20c. Your ability to manage conflict.   1   2   3   4   5

21c. Your ability to build a consensus.   1   2   3   4   5

22c. Your willingness to change when necessary.   1   2   3   4   5

23c. Your ability to communicate to others.   1   2   3   4   5

24c. Your ability to persuade/influence others.   1   2   3   4   5

25c. Your ability to lead others.   1   2   3   4   5

26c. Your ability to use power effectively.   1   2   3   4   5

27c. Your energy level.   1   2   3   4   5

28c. Your ability to work hard.   1   2   3   4   5

Open-Ended Questions

- The skills or abilities that helped you the most in this simulation were:

- The skills or abilities that helped you the least in this simulation were:

- As the simulation continued, I noticed that your behavior changed in the following ways:

- I noticed that you were at your best when:

- I noticed that you were especially helpful to:

General comments:

Organizational Frames Analysis:
A Tool to Enhance Leadership
John Sample and Martha C. Yopp

Summary

Modern organizations are complex and providing leadership within them that complements change and uncertainty requires the understanding of the multiple perspectives through which decisions are made. Four frames or perspectives are presented here and used to develop the Organizational Frames Analysis Questionnaire (OFAQ). These are the "structural" frame, the "human resource" frame, the "political" frame, and the "symbolic" or "cultural" frame.

Powerful forces in the environment characterize the turbulent condition of modern organizations; these include globalization, information technology, deregulation, and social/demographic changes. These forces foster rapid change, uncertainty, instability and, at times, organizational chaos. Change alters power relationships and undermines existing agreements and roles, causing confusion and distrust. People don't know what to expect from others. Conflict emerges among existing groups. Successful change requires that new concerns be identified and coalitions built so that key issues can be negotiated and solutions implemented quickly. People need support and encouragement as they let go of the old ways and accept new procedures, technologies, leaders, and/or symbols.

There is always more than one way to respond to any organizational problem or dilemma. Organizations, large and small, benefit if their leaders expand the options by relying on more than one perspective and also demonstrate the willingness to use multiple lenses.

Organizational Leadership

Decision makers frequently think and act in ways that limit their vision and impede their ability to understand and respond effectively to the complexities of our modern, constantly changing world. Some organizational leaders still rely on a *rational-technical* approach that is predicated on the idea that good management is about seizing and maintaining control over subordinates, rather than empowering them to accept the responsibility for identifying and implementing best practices themselves.

The reality is that, in today's fast-paced, global, changing society, no one is able to control others very successfully for very long. The autocratic system of management is dying, if not dead. Decision makers must learn to embrace an expressive-artistic management philosophy that encourages flexibility, creativity, self-sufficiency in others, and the development of individual and organizational consciousness or spirit (Bolman & Deal, 1991).

Artistry, when practiced in modern day organizations, is neither exact nor precise. The artful leader must interpret experience and express it in a way that arouses positive feelings and allows for emotion, subtlety, and ambiguity. Artful leadership enables people to envision new possibilities, new images, and a new vision. It promotes the building of supportive relationships and the concept of synergism to cultivate quality, commitment, and creativity within their respective organizations.

An analytical tool is presented here to help in the metamorphosis of modern organizations, the Organizational Frames Analysis Questionnaire (OFAQ). The questionnaire is based on the valuable contribution of reframing organizations by Bolman and Deal (1991).

Reframing Organizations

Bolman and Deal (1991) believe that higher order learning involves the development of "stencils" that frame and give meaning to experiences. Because they have multiple stencils or frames, people view situations in more than one way. This helps heighten intuition, gives an understanding of human dynamics, and improves decision making. Building on the premise of stencils, Bolman and Deal developed and refined four lenses or "frames" to use to better understand organizational behavior. These include:

- The Structural Frame
- The Human Resource Frame
- The Political Frame
- The Symbolic Frame

The Structural Frame

Our *structural frames* help us emphasize the importance of formal roles and relationships. Organizations create rules, policies, and chains of command to coordinate a wide range of activities. Managers may spend most of their time trying to determine how to divide the work—and then how best to put it back together again after it has been divided. Using the frame becomes ritualistic, whereas a more holistic approach might be preferable.

The Human Resource Frame

The *human resource frame* allows us to operate on the premise that organizations are made up of individuals who have needs, feelings, predispositions, and, in all likelihood, prejudices. Through this frame, we can see others as unique, having personality preferences, exhibiting strengths as well as deficiencies, and having the capacity to learn new things. However, these same people exhibit mistrust and resistance to change. The key to our effectiveness is to design organizations that value and embrace people and their abilities to get the job done and feel good about themselves and the organization at the same time. To this end, self-esteem and confidence should be enhanced.

The Political Frame

The *political frame* helps us view organizations as arenas in which different interest groups compete for power and scarce resources. Conflict is inevitable when one has this frame because we see only the differences in needs, perspectives, and lifestyles among individuals and groups. Coalitions form around special interests. Power can concentrate in the wrong places or become so broadly dispersed that it is almost impossible to do things in a timely fashion. Bargaining, negotiation, compromise, and even coercion are all a part of organizational life and are attempts to deal with this frame.

The Symbolic Frame

The *symbolic frame* allows us to look beyond assumptions of purely rational behavior and view organizations as tribes, theater, or carnivals. We can see organizations as cultures influenced as much by rituals, ceremonies, stories, heroes, and myth as by rules, human relations, or politics. In this context, organizations are like the theater. Various actors play out the drama inside the organization, while outside audiences form impressions based on what they see occurring on stage. Problems arise when ceremonies and rituals lose their mystique. Change and reform are promoted through the use of symbols, myths, drama, and metaphors that help formulate a vision and inspire a following.

Using Multiple Perspectives or Frames

Limited perspectives impede one's ability to understand and manage organizations. The inability to consider multiple perspectives undermines efforts to manage or change organizations. Relying on only one or two perspectives or frames reveals only part of the total picture. Each frame or perspective brings into focus a different and vital image that should not be overlooked.

Leaders tend to be able to use one or two frames, but not usually all four. By expanding their leadership horizons to include all four frames, they can become more reflective, thoughtful, and explicit about their own values and beliefs as well as insightful about the interpersonal and organizational dynamics around them. This helps them become more effective in riding the waves of change, visualizing new possibilities, and creating new opportunities. It is assumed that by using all four frames leaders will be better able to understand their own strengths, work to expand them, recognize and overcome deficiencies in themselves and others, and build teams that provide leadership and direction for the organization.

The Organizational Frames Analysis Questionnaire (OFAQ)

The OFAQ was conceptualized and designed to help consultants and organizational leaders understand and appreciate the power of organizational frame analysis for decision making and leadership. Heretofore, much of the theory and research on organizations has been dominated by one frame or another, but just viewing the organization through a single frame is not sufficient. Organizations contain multiple realities that must be recognized and addressed. Possessing multiple frames allows leaders to come much closer to being able to see the total picture.

As leaders chart new ground, they become personally challenged, and the people with whom they come into contact, both inside and outside the organization, become challenged also. The environment is energized and renewed. These leaders and their colleagues find their own distinctive voices and develop the ability to use multiple points of view intelligently and effectively. They tend to see that the old rules don't work anymore and that new ones are necessary. Leaders must continually examine and reexamine their own assumptions and those of other key stakeholders to eliminate blinders they may have that impede their vision or dampen the spirits of the whole organization.

The OFAQ can be used to assess individuals and groups on how they use the four frames identified by Bolman and Deal (1991). It provides feedback on the following processes: planning, decision making, reorganizing, evaluating, conflict, goal setting, communication, meetings, motivation, and leadership (see Table 1). The OFAQ might be used as part of an organization development intervention in which people working in various levels are surveyed and the results shared in ways that broaden respondents' own perspectives. Or it might be part of a leadership development program to demonstrate the power of multiple perspectives for more effective leadership.

Administration, Scoring, and Interpretation

Tell respondents that the OFAQ is designed to provide feedback about different frames of reference that leaders and managers within the organization may currently have. Ask them to read the instructions carefully. They will be asked to distribute four attributes for each preference using a 10-point scale. Respondents then complete the scoring form at the end of the questionnaire. Scores for the four frames—structural, human resources, political, and symbolic—are determined by summing each of the four columns.

Higher scores for any of the four frames indicate a relative preference for a particular frame or frames. Lower scores indicate a lower preference. Respondents are provided with a summary of each of the four frames for review. You may want to provide group-level feedback by function within an organization, by level within an organization, or by personnel status (management versus employees).

Reliability and Validity

The OAFQ was developed using a content validity strategy. Questionnaire items are based on the four organizational frames developed by Bolman and Deal (1991). Attempts to establish reliability are in progress.

Summary

The *structural* approach to management or leadership is vital, but is not enough. It takes the form of organizational charts, chains of command, procedure manuals, rules, contracts, personnel records, evaluation forms, and performance assessments. It includes everything that can be accurately reflected on paper: annual reports, statistical data, nuts and bolts, the bottom line.

The *human resources* approach looks specifically at the people who make up the organization. It recognizes that people are the organization's greatest asset and that they should be valued, recognized, rewarded, empowered, and celebrated. Indeed, people within the organization can and do impact the short-term and long-term success or failure of the organization. People who feel good about themselves in their working

Table 1. Four Interpretations of Organizational Processes

Process	Structural Frame	Human Resource Frame	Political Frame	Symbolic Frame
Planning	Strategies to set objectives and co-ordinate resources	Gatherings to promote participation	Arenas to air conflicts and realign power	Ritual to signal responsibility and produce symbols, negotiate meaning
Decision Making	Rational sequence to produce right decision	Open process to produce commitment	Opportunity to gain or exercise power	Ritual to provide comfort and support until decision happens
Reorganizing	Realign roles and responsibilities to fit tasks and environment	Maintain a balance between human needs and formal roles	Redistribute power and form new coalitions	Maintain an image of accountability and responsiveness; negotiate new social order
Evaluating	Way to distribute rewards or penal-ties and control performance	Process for helping individuals grow and improve	Opportunity to exercise power	Occasion to play roles in shared ritual
Approaching Conflict	Maintain organi-zational goals by having authorities resolve conflict	Develop relation-ships by having individual confront conflict	Develop power by bargaining, forcing, or manipulating other to win	Develop shared values and use conflict to negotiate meaning
Goal Setting	Keep organization headed in the right direction	Keep people in-volved and com-munication open	Provide oppor-tunity for people and groups to make interests known	Develop symbols and shared values
Communication	Transmit facts and information	Exchange informa-tion, needs, and feelings	Vehicles for influ-encing or manipu-lating others	Telling stories
Meetings	Formal occasions for making decisions	Informal occasions for involvement, sharing feelings	Competitive occasions to win points	Sacred occasions to celebrate and trans-form the culture
Motivation and Leadership	Economic incentives	Growth and self-actualization	Coercion, manipulation, and seduction	Symbols and celebrations

Based on work by Bolman and Deal (1991).

environment and who believe themselves to be an important part of a healthy organization are a powerful presence, but this frame in itself is not enough.

The *political* frame is useful to determine where the real power and control within the organization reside. Managers may have titles and be given authority, but these do not necessarily make them effective leaders. Grass roots power and influence may rest within the rank-and-file employees. Money also affects power. Those who have the gold tend to make the rules. In effective organizations the leaders and the followers operate in harmony and function as a team. However, this frame is not sufficient for success either.

The *symbolic* frame includes everything that permeates the culture of the organization. Organizations have personalities, traditions, expectations, and rituals. These are powerful, but are not always recognized as such. When, where, and how does an organization recognize and celebrate success? Are key people within the organization merely playing a part, or are they truly contributing to the health, strength, and sustainability of the whole? This frame is powerful and underlying much of what happens, but it is still not enough by itself.

Identifying elements within an organization that represent each of the four frames, bringing them to the forefront, and brainstorming how they help or hinder organizational success and stability can do much to improve overall organizational effectiveness. Learning to see the organizational world in all four ways can have a powerful effect.

Reference

Bolman, L.G., & Deal, T.E. (1991). *Reframing organizations: Artistry, choice, and leadership*. San Francisco, CA: Jossey-Bass.

John Sample *is a visiting assistant professor of adult education and human resource development in the College of Education at Florida State University, Tallahassee, Florida. He coordinates the M.S. degree and certificate program in human resource development. He is a recognized expert in legal liability and HRD and has published extensively, including in the Pfeiffer Annuals.*

Martha C. Yopp *is a professor in the adult and organizational learning program at the University of Idaho, Boise Center. She has been a professor of business education and office administration at the University of Idaho since 1986. She teaches and advises in the adult education and human resource development program. She also serves as the director of the University of Idaho Center for Economic Education.*

Organizational Frames Analysis Questionnaire (OFAQ)

John Sample and Martha C. Yopp

Different people may use different frames of reference to understand their organizations. The purpose of the OFAQ questionnaire is to provide information about the preferred frame of reference that you might utilize in understanding your organization.

The questionnaire is composed of ten preferences about managing. You are to read the four alternative statements for each of the ten preferences. Since each alternative statement is different, please select the alternatives *most* and *least* characteristic of you. Since there is no right or wrong way to manage or to think about an organization, the best response to each alternative statement is your own personal preference. Answer honestly, as only candid responses will provide you with useful information about yourself.

Instructions: From each of the four alternatives, select the one that is *most characteristic of you* and place the letter of that alternative at the point on the scale that reflects the *degree of preference* that you have for that statement. Next, select the preference that is *least characteristic of you* and place its letter on the appropriate place on the scale. Having found the most and least preference alternatives, place the letters of the remaining two alternatives within this range according to how characteristic each preference is for you.

For example, you might answer as follows for a set of four alternatives:

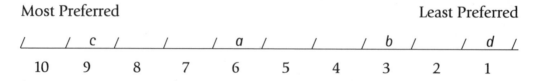

Most Preferred   Least Preferred

/	/ *c* /	/	/ *a* /	/	/ *b* /	/ *d* /
10	9	8	7	6	5	4	3	2	1

Now begin the process. You will have 15 minutes to complete the assessment.

1. I prefer to . . .
   a. develop strategies, set objectives, and coordinate resources
   b. promote gatherings that encourage participation
   c. encourage arenas to air conflicts and realign power
   d. promote rituals to signal responsibility, produce symbols, and negotiate meanings

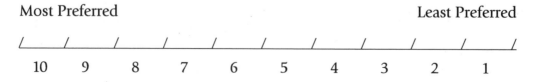

Most Preferred   Least Preferred

/	/	/	/	/	/	/	/	/	/
10	9	8	7	6	5	4	3	2	1

2. I prefer to . . .
   a. open the process of decision making to produce commitment
   b. provide comfort and support until a decision is made
   c. develop a rational sequence to produce the right decision
   d. have opportunities to gain and exercise power

   Most Preferred   Least Preferred

   / ___ / ___ / ___ / ___ / ___ / ___ / ___ / ___ / ___ / ___ /
     10   9   8   7   6   5   4   3   2   1

3. I prefer to . . .
   a. redistribute power and form new coalitions
   b. maintain an image of accountability and responsiveness and negotiate new social order
   c. maintain balance between human needs and formal roles
   d. realign roles and responsibilities to fit tasks and environment

   Most Preferred   Least Preferred

   / ___ / ___ / ___ / ___ / ___ / ___ / ___ / ___ / ___ / ___ /
     10   9   8   7   6   5   4   3   2   1

4. I prefer to . . .
   a. have occasions to play roles in shared rituals
   b. manage processes for helping individuals grow and improve
   c. find ways to distribute rewards or penalties and control performance
   d. have opportunities to exercise my power in the distribution of rewards

   Most Preferred   Least Preferred

   / ___ / ___ / ___ / ___ / ___ / ___ / ___ / ___ / ___ / ___ /
     10   9   8   7   6   5   4   3   2   1

5. I prefer to . . .
   a. maintain organizational goals by having authorities resolve conflict
   b. develop relationships by having individuals confront conflict
   c. develop shared values and use conflict to negotiate meaning
   d. develop power by bargaining, forcing, or manipulating others to win

   Most Preferred   Least Preferred

   / ___ / ___ / ___ / ___ / ___ / ___ / ___ / ___ / ___ / ___ /
     10   9   8   7   6   5   4   3   2   1

6. I prefer to . . .
   a. develop symbols and shared values
   b. provide opportunities for individuals and groups to make their interests known
   c. keep people involved and communication open
   d. keep the organization headed in the right direction

Most Preferred   Least Preferred

/_____/_____/_____/_____/_____/_____/_____/_____/_____/_____/
   10   9   8   7   6   5   4   3   2   1

7. I prefer to . . .
   a. transmit facts and information
   b. provide vehicles for influencing or manipulating others
   c. tell stories that exemplify core values and beliefs
   d. exchange information, needs, and feelings

Most Preferred   Least Preferred

/_____/_____/_____/_____/_____/_____/_____/_____/_____/_____/
   10   9   8   7   6   5   4   3   2   1

8. I prefer . . .
   a. informal occasions for involvement, sharing feelings
   b. competitive occasions to win points
   c. formal occasions for making decisions
   d. shared occasions to celebrate and transform the culture

Most Preferred   Least Preferred

/_____/_____/_____/_____/_____/_____/_____/_____/_____/_____/
   10   9   8   7   6   5   4   3   2   1

9. I prefer . . .
   a. economic incentives
   b. growth and self-actualization
   c. control, order, and compliance
   d. symbols and celebrations

Most Preferred   Least Preferred

/_____/_____/_____/_____/_____/_____/_____/_____/_____/_____/
   10   9   8   7   6   5   4   3   2   1

10. I prefer the role of . . .
   a. supporter, empowerer, catalyst
   b. advocate, coalition builder, coach
   c. visionary, provider of inspiration, prophet
   d. developer of policies, procedures, analyst, designer

Most Preferred   Least Preferred

/____/____/____/____/____/____/____/____/____/____/
   10   9   8   7   6   5   4   3   2   1

Scoring

By placing your preferences on the 10-point scale, you have weighted each item according to the utility that each item has for you. To score the Organizational Frames Questionnaire, simply take the number value over which you placed an item letter as the score for that item. See example below.

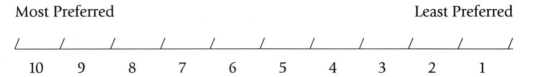

Most Preferred   Least Preferred

/____/_a_/____/____/_c_/____/____/_b_/____/_d_/
   10   9   8   7   6   5   4   3   2   1

The score for "a" would be 9, for "c" would be 6, and so on. Go back through the survey and determine your scores for each item and enter them in the spaces provided below. Note that the preference items are *not* in alphabetical order; they have been arranged according to four management frames that have been identified by Bolman and Deal (1991). Proceed carefully to locate and record accurately the scores you have indicated on the survey form.

		Structural	Human Resource	Political	Symbolic
1.	Planning	a. _____	b. _____	c. _____	d. _____
2.	Decision Making	c. _____	a. _____	d. _____	b. _____
3.	Reorganizing	d. _____	c. _____	a. _____	b. _____
4.	Evaluating	a. _____	b. _____	c. _____	d. _____
5.	Conflict	a. _____	b. _____	d. _____	c. _____
6.	Goal Setting	d. _____	c. _____	b. _____	a. _____

		Structural	Human Resource	Political	Symbolic
7.	Communication	a. _____	c. _____	b. _____	d. _____
8.	Meetings	c. _____	a. _____	b. _____	d. _____
9.	Motivation	a. _____	b. _____	c. _____	d. _____
10.	Leadership	d. _____	b. _____	a. _____	c. _____
	Totals =	_____	_____	_____	_____

Summary of Bolman and Deal's Four Frames

The *structural* frame emphasizes the importance of formal roles and relationships. The structural frame reminds us that most people within organizations are able to accept structure, rules, and regulations as they attempt to do their jobs the best way they know how. Leaders who have this frame tend to focus only on clarifying goals, developing a structure to solve problems,, accomplishing a task, or implementing an idea within the organizational environment. They sometimes fail because they underestimate the resistance they will encounter when they don't build a base of support for their actions.

The *human resource* frame operates on the premise that organizations are made up of individuals who have needs, feelings, and sometimes prejudices. The human resource frame reminds us that people are complex. They have needs, feelings, personalities, ideas, and egos. They are adaptable, but sometimes resistant to change, and they respond best when treated with respect and as important individuals. Leaders who use primarily the human resource frame believe in empowerment and support, and they communicate that belief. The dignity and worth of the individual are very important parts of their processes. Human resource leaders tend to be visible and accessible under this organizational frame.

The *political* frame views organizations as arenas in which different interest groups compete for power and scarce resources. The political frame reminds us that resources are always scarce and that individuals and groups will fight over resource allocations. Power and politics are always present and cannot be overlooked or ignored. Leaders who promote a political frame clarify what they want and what they can get. They build linkages to other stakeholders. They focus on recognizing constituencies, building networks and bridges to leadership, and managing conflict as productively as possible. They persuade first, negotiate second, and use coercion only when necessary. They may use power sparingly, but no one doubts they have it.

Those who hold the *symbolic* frame abandon the assumptions of rationality and treat organizations as tribes, theater, or carnivals. Leaders with this frame remind us of the extent to which reality is socially constructed and symbolically mediated. Meaning, the most important aspect of any human event, is viewed through the leader's own beliefs and values. In instances where multiple cultures intersect and important issues are ambiguous, we find that the symbolic process is vital. Leaders who favor symbolic leadership are inspirational and passionate. They may use dramatic and visible symbols as tactics for aligning employee behaviors and attitudes with the leader's vision and mission. They are transformative leaders who bring out the best in their followers and who move them to accomplish more for themselves and for the organization. It is not uncommon for these leaders to create slogans, tell stories, hold rallies, give awards, appear where they are least expected, and manage by wandering around.

Reference

Bolman, L.G., & Deal, T.E. (1991). *Reframing organizations: Artistry, choice, and leader-ship.* San Francisco, CA: Jossey-Bass.

The Web–Based Learning Readiness Inventory (WLRI):
Is Your Organization Ready for the Information Superhighway?

Douglas J. Swiatkowski and Amy Pawlusiak

Summary

The Web-Based Learning Readiness Inventory (WLRI) provides organizations a way to gauge their readiness to embark on an e-learning strategy. By completing the WLRI and interpreting the resulting data, an organization can make a more informed decision about whether to move ahead with web-based learning or not.

We live in a world driven by the technology of the day. Be it in automobiles, consumer electronics, or the service economy, technology is driving our efforts. As a society we need to reverse this dynamic, nowhere more evident than in the current drive to have training delivered via the web.

The push to put training on the web is more often a desire than a need. Even when web-based learning is identified as a real business need, many organizations fail to take into account what is needed to make the process efficient and successful. As Reinhard Zeigler of *eLearning* magazine states, learners often pay for the lack of preparation in that "well-intentioned managers and designers so totally fall in love with designing and building that they get disconnected from those who are stuck trying to use their stuff" (Ziegler, 2002).

In addition, it has been the authors' experience that few organizations bother to see whether web-based learning is what the target audience wants or is able to use. Shackleton-Jones (2002) summed it up well in saying, "e-Learning generally lacks both a sound technological and educational footing—summed up in the stick-the-information-on-the-Web approach. However, the choice of technologies is not nearly as important a consideration as are the learners and the ways in which they learn: they like to explore, see the relevance, take part, have choices, exchange information, be entertained, and so on.

"Almost any technology can be used to construct a well-formed learning system if the people involved in the deployment have an understanding of what constitutes learning. However, the widespread failure of e-learning suppliers to adopt new technologies or develop effective instructional design methodologies has forced businesses to blend their e-learning with instructor-led training in order to offer an acceptable solution."

Hence, the Web-Based Learning Readiness Inventory (WLRI) provides organizations a way to gauge their readiness to embark on an e-learning strategy. This tool is consistent with the recommendations of Beer (2000) that an assessment, or actually a number of them, need to be undertaken before moving forward into a web-based learning environment.

Through experience, interviews, and research, the authors have identified three key areas where an organization should look before starting an e-learning effort. In each of these areas, responses to fifteen distinct statements help to assess an organization's readiness for web-based learning.

The Instrument

The WLRI does not have a theoretical base but springs from a practical need. Both authors have witnessed web-based learning rollouts in organizations ill-prepared to do so. The ramifications have been poor courses, an inability to track user progress and success, user confusion, technical issues, and high costs due to the inability to develop materials in-house.

The WLRI forces an organization to look at three key components of a web-based learning environment:

1. The organization's technical readiness;

2. The organization's readiness to produce web-based learning; and

3. The organization's understanding, or lack thereof, of the target audience's needs and abilities.

By completing the WLRI and interpreting the resulting data, an organization can make a more informed decision about whether to move ahead with web-based learning or not. They will know where the costs will lie: in equipment, developing skill sets, or acquiring qualified developers. The organization will also be able to see its strengths and be able to leverage those.

Description of the Instrument

The WLRI is broken into three sections, each intended for a different audience. These are as follows:

1. Technical Readiness: The organization's information technology personnel.

2. Production Readiness: The organization's training personnel.

3. Target Audience Readiness: The targeted users of the web-based learning applications.

Each group responds to fifteen statements using a 5-point Likert scale, ranging from "strongly disagree" to "strongly agree." Each of the five selections has a corresponding numerical value ranging from –2 to 2, including zero. The inventory is self-scoring.

The Scoring Process

Once the questionnaires are completed and the data compiled (described later) a final number is calculated for each of the three sections. These numbers correspond to points on the scoring sheet for each section and create a Readiness Continuum. Placement on this continuum shows the organization's readiness visually.

Interpretation

Interpretation sheets help the user to see that placement far to the left, for example, indicates a lack of readiness and also means certain expenses to prepare. Placement far to the right, on the other hand, indicates a higher degree of readiness and that the organization can leverage its strengths when rolling out web-based learning.

Administration

Administration of the instrument is straightforward. First, identify members of the three audiences who will fill out the inventory. In the case of the target users, a random sampling is acceptable if size is an issue.

Once you have identified them, send potential audience members a memo or email informing them of the WLRI and the purposes for taking it. This memo should touch on the fact that the organization is looking at web-based learning as an option, that the potential respondent's input is critical to this decision, and that all responses will be kept in the strictest confidence. Include a reasonable deadline for completing and returning the inventory. Remind the users that the inventory is self-scoring and not to forget that important step.

Theory

Because this is not a theory-based tool, but a practical one, there is no need to present the theory behind it. However, respondents should know that if the organization were to proceed without considering their responses it could spell disaster for a web-based learning strategy.

There is no reason for participants to predict how they will score. It is only important to compile individual responses and convert them to a single number for each of the three groups completing the inventory.

Individual Scoring

The self-scoring process is quite simple. At the bottom of the page is a space for respondents to enter how many times they answered a particular way, either strongly disagree, disagree, neutral, agree, or strongly agree. They should multiply the numerical values of strongly disagree responses by a –2, disagrees by a –1, neutral by 0, agree responses by 1 and strongly agree by 2. Once they have done this, the respondents simply add across columns to arrive at a final number, which could be any number between –30 and +30.

Composite Score

You will do the final computation of the data to arrive at a composite score for each of the three groups. First, discard the highest and lowest scores to eliminate any bias. Then simply average the remaining responses. Be sure that N = original number received minus 2 (to account for the highest and lowest scores that were dropped). You will plot this composite score for each group on the WLRI Composite Scoring Sheet.

Interpretation

Interpretation is easy because the scores are plotted on a continuum. In each case (technical, production, and target user readiness), the farther to the right the composite score, the more ready that area is for web-based learning. The opposite is true for scores on the far left, which show a lack of readiness. The inventory itself contains an interpretation sheet, which looks at different combinations of scores and what they might mean in regard to readiness and costs and offering some possible reasons behind the score combinations.

Posting Scores

It is not important to post the WLRI scores, but it is a good idea to share the results with those who took part in the effort, as these scores help to justify any number of decisions that an organization needs to make when moving to a web-based learning environment—or in deciding not to do so at this time.

Other Uses

This inventory could also be used as a checklist once the decision has been made to move into a web-based learning environment. This will ensure that all areas identified as lacking are addressed.

Reliability and Validity

This instrument has not undergone a validation process at this time. It has, however, been presented to a number of professionals in the web-based learning field, in both technical and development arenas, and has been modified in order to obtain agreement that the tool will add value if used.

References

Beer, V. (2000) *The web learning fieldbook: Using the world wide web to build workplace learning environments.* San Francisco, CA: Pfeiffer.

Shackleton-Jones, N. (2002, November 14). The rationale behind the introduction of e-learning. *elearning.com* article ID 38367. Retrieved January 13, 2003, from www.elearningmag.com/elearning/article/articleDetail.jsp?id=41963

Ziegler, R. (2002, December 1). What's wrong with distance learning. *elearning.com* article ID 41963. Retrieved January 16, 2003 from www.elearningmag.com/elearning/article/articleDetail.jsp?id=41963

Douglas Swiatkowski *has been an instructional designer/ performance consultant for over ten years. He holds a master's degree in instructional technology from Wayne State University, Detroit, Michigan, where he earned the Outstanding Instructional Technology Master's Student Award for 1998. He is currently working toward his Ph.D. at Wayne State.*

Amy Pawlusiak *has been working in the field of instructional technology since 1997. She designed and developed stand-up training courses for the automotive industry until 1999, then designed e-learning exclusively. She is currently completing her master's degree at Wayne State University in education, specializing in instructional technology, and works for Macomb Community College, assisting faculty to incorporate technology into their on-ground and on-line classrooms.*

The Web–Based Learning Readiness Inventory (WLRI)

Douglas J. Swiatkowski and Amy Pawlusiak

The three inventories that follow will help you to check your organization's readiness for web-based learning.

WLRI Technical Readiness Tool

Audience: The Organization's Information Technology (IT) Employees

Instructions: Please take a few moments to complete and score the following brief inventory. Do so by reading the statement to the left and indicating your level of agreement by circling the choice that corresponds to one of the following levels of agreement:

SD = Strongly Disagree   D = Disagree   N = Neutral   A = Agree   SA = Strongly Agree

When you have finished, follow the scoring directions.

Statement

Server issues have been resolved so the courses have a place to be hosted.	SD	D	N	A	SA
The organization has a learning management system (LMS) to track students' web learning usage.	SD	D	N	A	SA
IT staff are ready to assist with providing a network learning management system (LMS) that would create course catalogs, schedules, and student registrations and also capture learner profile data.	SD	D	N	A	SA
The organization has committed to purchasing an off-the-shelf LMS.	SD	D	N	A	SA
The organization has committed to developing its own internal LMS.	SD	D	N	A	SA
IT staff would administer the database that stores information on courses and students.	SD	D	N	A	SA
IT staff are prepared to research technological standards for online learning and to counsel management accordingly.	SD	D	N	A	SA
IT staff are prepared to work with the training employees/group to ensure that online learning is accessible to employees with disabilities.	SD	D	N	A	SA

SD = Strongly Disagree   D = Disagree   N =Neutral   A = Agree   SA = Strongly Agree

Statement

Statement					
The information technology department has people knowledgeable in the technology behind web-based course serving or hosting.	SD	D	N	A	SA
Bandwidth issues of the end user's machines have been analyzed.	SD	D	N	A	SA
IT is willing to create (or already has) a help desk to support learners and training staff when computer problems arise.	SD	D	N	A	SA
IT is willing to support learners and training staff with technological issues such as hardware breakage, software corruption, and general network problems whenever they arise (24/7).	SD	D	N	A	SA
IT management is supportive of online learning and is convinced it will benefit ALL of the organization's employees.	SD	D	N	A	SA
IT staff are ready to be trained to successfully roll out and maintain an LMS.	SD	D	N	A	SA
The organization has committed to fill skill gaps either with employee training or by hiring skilled individuals.	SD	D	N	A	SA

Scoring

Instructions: Count the number of times you selected each choice and enter that number in the space below as shown in the example. Then do the calculations noted for each response. Total the numbers for your composite score.

	# of Responses	Calculation	Total
SD	5	Multiply by 2, assign negative value to total	−10
D	2	Multiply by 1, assign negative value to total	−2
N	1	Total is automatically zero	0
A	4	Multiply by 1, assign positive value to total	4
SA	3	Multiply by 2, assign positive value to total	6
		Composite total =	−2

Now complete the chart below by filling in your responses.

	# of Responses	Calculation	Total
SD		Multiply by 2, assign negative value to total	
D		Multiply by 1, assign negative value to total	
N		Total is automatically zero	
A		Multiply by 1, assign positive value to total	
SA		Multiply by 2, assign positive value to total	
		Composite total =	

WLRI Production Readiness Tool

Audience: The Organization's Training Employees

Instructions: Notice that there are two separate inventories below, "In-House Production" and "Outsourcing." Use the guidelines below to decide which one to complete.

- If your organization has decided to develop the web-based learning products in house, complete the In-House Inventory.

- If your organization has decided to outsource development of the web-based learning products, complete the Outsourced Inventory.

- If your organization has not yet made a decision on who will produce the web-based learning products, complete BOTH inventories.

In whichever case, read the statement to the left and indicate your level of agreement by circling the choice that corresponds to one of the following levels of agreement. When you are finished, see the scoring directions.

SD = Strongly Disagree   D = Disagree   N =Neutral   A = Agree   SA = Strongly Agree

In-House Development

Statement

Statement					
The organization has decided on which development product to use (Authorware®, Dreamweaver®, Front Page®, and so on).	SD	D	N	A	SA
The training department has people with web-based instructional design skills.	SD	D	N	A	SA
The training department has graphic and programming expertise.	SD	D	N	A	SA
The training department has processes for review and piloting of web-based courses that may be developed.	SD	D	N	A	SA
The training department has people knowledgeable in the technology behind web-based course serving or hosting.	SD	D	N	A	SA

SD = Strongly Disagree   D = Disagree   N =Neutral   A = Agree   SA = Strongly Agree

Statement

Statement					
Management is firmly behind in-house development of online learning solutions.	SD	D	N	A	SA
Our training department/group has a long-term plan to enter the computer-based learning arena.	SD	D	N	A	SA
Training staff understands the differences between online learning and informational needs of an employee.	SD	D	N	A	SA
Training staff is prepared to attend courses that teach how to use the LMS chosen.	SD	D	N	A	SA
I either know, or would be willing to learn, how to use software tools that would enable me to create online courses.	SD	D	N	A	SA
There is management support (monetary and vocal) for a web-based learning initiative.	SD	D	N	A	SA
Management realizes it will take several years for web-based learning to become established.	SD	D	N	A	SA
I am personally committed to web-based learning as a solution for our organization.	SD	D	N	A	SA
I am committed to seeking feedback (assessments) from our audience of learners in order to continually update and improve online instruction.	SD	D	N	A	SA
The training department has people literate in the selected development product.	SD	D	N	A	SA

Scoring

Instructions: Count the number of times you selected each choice and enter that number in the space below as shown in the example. Then do the calculations noted for each response. Total the numbers for your composite score.

	# of Responses	Calculation	Total
SD	5	Multiply by 2, assign negative value to total	–10
D	2	Multiply by 1, assign negative value to total	–2
N	1	Total is automatically zero	0
A	4	Multiply by 1, assign positive value to total	4
SA	3	Multiply by 2, assign positive value to total	6
		Composite total =	–2

Now complete the chart below by filling in your responses.

	# of Responses	Calculation	Total
SD		Multiply by 2, assign negative value to total	
D		Multiply by 1, assign negative value to total	
N		Total is automatically zero	
A		Multiply by 1, assign positive value to total	
SA		Multiply by 2, assign positive value to total	
		Composite total =	

Outsourced Development

SD = Strongly Disagree   D = Disagree   N =Neutral   A = Agree   SA = Strongly Agree

Statement

The organization has developed technical and design standards to share with a selected vendor.	SD	D	N	A	SA
The organization has already explored the various vendors available to develop the courses.	SD	D	N	A	SA
The organization has already budgeted funds for the outsourced development of web-based courses.	SD	D	N	A	SA
The organization has decided what the final deliverable from the vendors will be (for example, courses only, courses installed and set up, follow-up, revisions, and so forth).	SD	D	N	A	SA
The organization has benchmarked other organizations that are using vendors to gauge the quality of their work and services.	SD	D	N	A	SA
The organization has defined who the internal interface(s) with the vendor(s) will be.	SD	D	N	A	SA
The organization has decided who will handle the project management function (internal person or vendor).	SD	D	N	A	SA
We have a change management plan ready to support the launch of web-based learning.	SD	D	N	A	SA
The organization has benchmarked other organizations to learn how the vendor(s) work with internal personnel.	SD	D	N	A	SA
The organization has someone with the proper knowledge to make a decision on this type of vendor(s).	SD	D	N	A	SA
There is management support (monetary and vocal) for an outsourced web-based learning initiative.	SD	D	N	A	SA

SD = Strongly Disagree   D = Disagree   N =Neutral   A = Agree   SA = Strongly Agree

Statement

| We are prepared to deal with the varying web-based learning solutions in the marketplace and are knowledgeable about the industry. | SD | D | N | A | SA |

We are prepared to deal with the varying web-based learning solutions in the marketplace and are knowledgeable about the industry.   SD   D   N   A   SA

I have experience in working with outside vendors.   SD   D   N   A   SA

I am personally committed to web-based learning as a solution for our organization.   SD   D   N   A   SA

I am committed to seeking feedback from our audience of learners in order to continually update and improve online instruction options.   SD   D   N   A   SA

Scoring

Instructions: Count the number of times you selected each choice and enter that number in the space below, as shown in the example. Then do the calculations noted for each response. Total the numbers for your composite score.

	# of Responses	Calculation	Total
SD	5	Multiply by 2, assign negative value to total	−10
D	2	Multiply by 1, assign negative value to total	−2
N	1	Total is automatically zero	0
A	4	Multiply by 1, assign positive value to total	4
SA	3	Multiply by 2, assign positive value to total	6
		Composite total =	−2

Now complete the chart below by filling in your responses.

	# of Responses	Calculation	Total
SD		Multiply by 2, assign negative value to total	
D		Multiply by 1, assign negative value to total	
N		Total is automatically zero	
A		Multiply by 1, assign positive value to total	
SA		Multiply by 2, assign positive value to total	
		Composite total =	

WLRI Target Audience Readiness Tool

Audience: The organization's target users (If number is large, a representative sample is acceptable.)

Instructions: Please take a few moments to complete and score the following brief inventory. Do so by reading the statement to the left and indicating your level of agreement by circling the choice that corresponds to one of the following levels of agreement:

SD = Strongly Disagree   D = Disagree   N =Neutral   A = Agree   SA = Strongly Agree

When you are finished, see the scoring directions.

Statement

I have experience in using web-based training.	SD	D	N	A	SA
I have been requesting web-based training courses.	SD	D	N	A	SA
Our organization lacks training that is accessible easily from home or the workplace.	SD	D	N	A	SA
I would utilize training offered to me via the Internet.	SD	D	N	A	SA
I am very comfortable using technologies such as Windows® (or any other operating system on a computer).	SD	D	N	A	SA
I use the Internet/intranet daily and am comfortable with the online tools needed to access them.	SD	D	N	A	SA
I see a need for other types of training besides the regular in-house/stand-up training offered to me.	SD	D	N	A	SA
I am ready for a different type of learning environment where the instructor may be more of a virtual facilitator or mentor.	SD	D	N	A	SA
I believe I am ready to use training offered on the computer/online.	SD	D	N	A	SA
I would receive support from my manager if I were to take online training courses.	SD	D	N	A	SA

SD = Strongly Disagree   D = Disagree   N =Neutral   A = Agree   SA = Strongly Agree

Statement

Web instruction can be as valuable as being in a live group setting with other people for discussions.	SD	D	N	A	SA
I want online learning to be offered to me in this organization, and would use it.	SD	D	N	A	SA
I see the benefits of online learning.	SD	D	N	A	SA
I find the idea of taking an online training course interesting.	SD	D	N	A	SA
I believe I can learn by using online training courses.	SD	D	N	A	SA

Scoring

Instructions: Count the number of times you selected each choice and enter that number in the space below, as shown in the example. Then do the calculations noted for each response. Total the numbers for your composite score.

	# of Responses	Calculation	Total
SD	5	Multiply by 2, assign negative value to total	−10
D	2	Multiply by 1, assign negative value to total	−2
N	1	Total is automatically zero	0
A	4	Multiply by 1, assign positive value to total	4
SA	3	Multiply by 2, assign positive value to total	6
		Composite total =	−2

Now complete the chart below by filling in your responses.

	# of Responses	Calculation	Total
SD		Multiply by 2, assign negative value to total	
D		Multiply by 1, assign negative value to total	
N		Total is automatically zero	
A		Multiply by 1, assign positive value to total	
SA		Multiply by 2, assign positive value to total	
		Composite total =	

WLRI Composite Scoring Sheet

Instructions: Following the example below, plot the composite scores you computed on each of the readiness inventories on the graph below, using the example below as a guide. Remember, you may not need to use both Production Readiness scores. When all of your composite scores are plotted, connect them with a colored marker. This is your Organizational Web-Learning Readiness Profile.

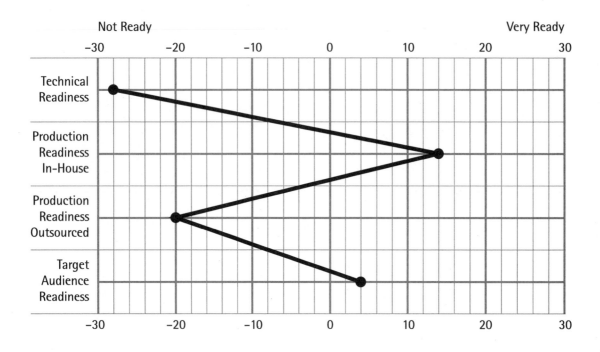

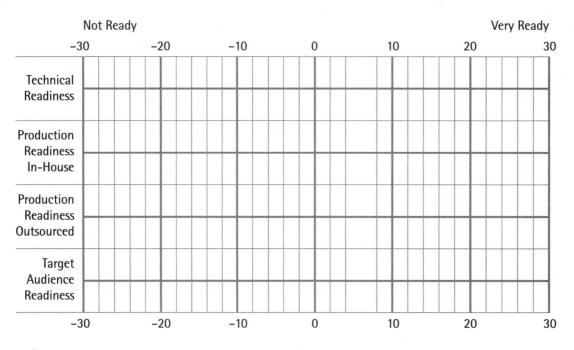

WLRI Interpretation Sheet

Technical Readiness

Scores in the negative numbers indicate a deficiency in either hardware or the necessary people skills in your organization's information technology staff. Both of these issues are very costly to overcome. These results should not dissuade you from moving on with web-based training, but you should examine the budget available for the effort. If your scores are positive, it shows that you have many of the technical and people aspects covered. The further to the right the scores are, the less you will need to invest here and the more you will be able to leverage your effort.

Production Readiness

Note: If your organization has not yet decided whether to develop in-house or outsource, the results can guide your decision by showing where your in-house strengths or weaknesses lie, as well as your information base and readiness to bring in outside vendors.

In-House Development

If your organization scored far to the left in this category, you may want to rethink the strategy of in-house development. It will be costly to bring your training personnel up-to-speed on the necessary technologies to develop the training in-house. The score may even reveal a need to bring on additional design or technical staff. A score far to the right shows that your organization does have the skill base it needs to develop web-based learning in-house.

Outsourced Development

In this category, a score far to the left reveals two things. First, It shows that your organization has not done a great deal of homework to identify possible vendors and investigate costs associated with them. It also indicates that your organization has not taken some key steps necessary to ensure that, once selected, a vendor will be able to work quickly and efficiently, based on well-defined developmental and technical standards. Scores to the right reveal that your organization may be ready to pursue vendors in order to establish a relationship. This is especially true if your organization has not decided between in-house and outsourced and your in-house scores were in the negatives.

Target Audience Readiness

Truly this category is the key to a successful web-based learning effort, even if you have very positive scores on the other readiness indicators. Scores to the left here show that your users are not ready or are not open to web-based learning. Conversely, high scores, or scores far to the right, in this category may convince your organizational management to invest the time and dollars to overcome shortfalls in the other categories.

Remember, these are guidelines for interpretation. Discussion and planning need to take place based on this data before you dismiss or embrace any web-based effort. Just as a thermometer only tells a doctor that a patient is running a fever without telling why, the WLRI results only tell you the organization's level of readiness, not why it is at that level.

Introduction
to the Articles and Discussion Resources Section

The Articles and Discussion Resources Section is a collection of materials useful to every facilitator. The theories, background information, models, and methods will challenge facilitators' thinking, enrich their professional development, and assist their internal and external clients with productive change. These articles may be used as a basis for lecturettes, as handouts in training sessions, or as background reading material.

This section will provide you with a variety of useful ideas, theoretical opinions, teachable models, practical strategies, and proven intervention methods. The articles will add richness and depth to your training and consulting knowledge and skills. They will challenge you to think differently, explore new concepts, and experiment with new interventions. The articles will continue to add a fresh perspective to your work.

The 2004 Pfeiffer Annual: Consulting includes five articles, in the following categories:

Communication: Feedback

Coaching: Using Feedback to Achieve Desired Performance,
by Stacey L. Gannon and Darlene Van Tiem

Communication: Coaching and Encouraging

Life-Centering Stories: A Powerful Coaching and Self-Discovery Tool,
by Aviv Shahar

Consulting: Organizations: Their Characteristics and How They Function

Positioning to Create Customer Value Through the Systems Thinking Approach,
by Stephen G. Haines

Consulting: Consulting Strategies and Techniques

Organizational Success Through Collaborative Consulting,
by Neil J. Simon and James E. Agnew

Leadership: Top-Management Issues and Concerns

Change the Snapshot: Change Perceptions, by Marcia Ruben
and Jan M. Schmuckler

As with previous *Annuals,* this volume covers a wide variety of topics. The range of articles presented encourages thought-provoking discussion about the present and future of HRD. Other articles on specific subjects can be located by using our comprehensive *Reference Guide to Handbooks and Annuals.* The guide is updated regularly and indexes the contents of all the *Annuals* and the *Handbooks of Structured Experiences.* With each revision, the *Reference Guide* becomes a complete, up-to-date, and easy-to-use resource for selecting appropriate materials from the *Annuals* and *Handbooks.* A print version of the *Reference Guide* is available for volumes through 1999. An online supplement covering the years through 2003 can be found at www.pfeiffer. com/go/supplement.

Here, and in the *Reference Guide,* we have done our best to categorize the articles for easy reference; however, many of the articles encompass a range of topics, disciplines, and applications. If you do not find what you are looking for under one category, check a related category. In some cases we may place an article in the "Training" *Annual* that also has implications for "Consulting," and vice versa. As the field of HRD continues to grow and develop, there is more and more crossover between training and consulting. Explore all the contents of both volumes of the *Annual* in order to realize the full potential for learning and development that each offers.

Coaching:
Using Feedback to Achieve Desired Performance
Stacey L. Gannon and Darlene Van Tiem

Summary

Coaching has become a vogue term for hands-on performance management in today's organizations. Many performance consultants and management experts are jumping on the bandwagon to develop and provide coaching solutions for companies hungry to drive results through the efforts of their employees. However, the success of coaching interventions requires more than just a model solution. A demonstrated organizational commitment to human performance improvement theory and process provides the proper environment for coaching efforts to prosper. This article examines a best-practice approach to coaching, in which the act of coaching serves as the anchor for performance improvement.

"Near 50 percent increases in return on assets and return on equity, over a twenty-four-month period" is hard to argue with as a dramatic statement of performance improvement. Add to that "record growth in core product sales" and you are sure to please all stakeholders. Such has been the case for a Midwestern bank holding company since coaching became the driver for its sales management business model.

A customized version of the model that follows, specific to a selling environment, was piloted in select markets from 1999 through 2001. Currently the model is being expanded across all markets and lines of business because of its proven results.

Defining Coaching in a Business Environment

According to *The Oxford Desk Dictionary,* coaching is the act of instructing or training in a sport. Ask any executive how he or she defines coaching and the answer might be something akin to "managing people to succeed" or "driving human performance." In human performance improvement terms, coaching is a stimulus for impacting the work environment by providing information through "relevant and frequent feedback on the adequacy of performance" (Gilbert, 1978, p. 88).

Research has shown that a lack of information and feedback ranks consistently high among workers as a leading cause of poor performance (Dean, 1994, p. 25). The fact is that coaching is a means to an end. In business, that "end" is likely to be the desired business results or performance requirements. Properly aligned, coaching is an appropriate intervention when lack of feedback affects behavior and accomplishment and the result is less-than-desired performance.

An effective coaching model incorporates management commitment, proper accountabilities and metrics, training, communication, incentives, and, most importantly, nonnegotiable discipline. Once implemented and proven effective, the model can continue to be used as a diagnostic tool to identify opportunities for improvement and best practices.

The model described here assumes that "coach" is synonymous with manager or supervisor. The target of a coaching interaction, for purposes of this discussion, is a direct report or work team, and the objective of coaching would be to improve performance of individual employees and work teams in order to accomplish desired business results.

A Model Approach

Figure 1 shows our model, which centers coaching among four performance system components: *management commitment, incentives, metrics,* and *communication.* These four elements make up the performance system in any organization. Although the elements, alignment, and effectiveness of the performance system may vary, these components are essential to coaching success.

It is essential that the four components be properly aligned with business objectives and all other elements of the organization's performance system so that the value of coaching can be maximized. The path to success begins with a commitment from executive management.

Management Commitment

First, the coaching model must be accepted and agreed on by the executive team. Then they must set expectations for where they want to take the organization. The best place to start is by answering the question: "What business results do we want to achieve?"

Figure 1. A Coaching Model

The next step is to design *nonnegotiable coaching and performance standards* for all employees. Such standards are critical to driving performance.

After the coaching model and performance standards are fully defined, management must focus on how to introduce the coaching initiative and what it will take to sustain it. They must also commit to providing the necessary *resources* to ensure success. The entire system must be in *alignment*, understanding what the new expectations are, why they are necessary, what will have to happen differently and when, and how to proceed. Staff will want to know: "What's in it for me?" Resources must be dedicated to supporting the communication effort, training staff on how to complete their nonnegotiable performance standards, providing appropriate incentives to motivate desired behaviors, and tracking results.

This model assumes that managers will spend at least 80 percent of their time fulfilling their nonnegotiable coaching requirements; thus, work teams must be balanced so that coaches have a manageable number of direct reports. In short, following the model is no small undertaking, but when it is properly aligned and effectively implemented, the return on investment can be tremendous.

Once resources have been allocated and a full commitment to the coaching model has been made, the executive team should roll out the model in a top-down format. The training begins with the members of executive management, as they become the first to "learn how to do it." Executive and senior managers must act as "head coaches" and model the expected behaviors for their direct reports and work teams. The nonnegotiable coaching and performance standards apply to everyone in the organization, executives included.

The training effort should include opportunities to practice actual coaching interactions in a safe environment. This enables trainers to give *coaching feedback* to participants during the learning process. Further, participants must complete post-training transfer of their skills to the job and begin using what they have learned. Because the process is rolled out "top down," executive and senior managers, now known as "senior coaches," are assigned to audit post-training coaching sessions run by line managers in order to provide further feedback and instructions and to strengthen skills. This process, known as "field coaching," is ongoing to ensure continuous improvement and identify best practices. Field coaching is one of the nonnegotiable performance standards for senior and executive managers, with a minimum number of field coaching activities required over a given period of time.

Incentives

To maximize the value of coaching efforts, some form of comprehensive incentive plan needs to be in place, be thoroughly understood, and be communicated effectively. As we learned from Gilbert (1978) and others, incentives and other motivators influence performance. Also, consequences for non-performers must be communicated clearly. *It is important that the result, whether negative or positive, be linked with the behavior that earned it.* It is also essential that the executive team add in the costs associated with incentives when making the commitment to the coaching model.

The management team must be aware of a pitfall commonly encountered when using incentives. As stated earlier, the objective of coaching is *to improve the performance of individual employees and work teams in order to accomplish desired business results.* Often, coaches find it easier to motivate employees by "dangling the carrot," rather than pushing for continuous improvement that exceeds expectations. The key is to coach toward performance that meets the needs of the organization, not to meet the needs of the employee who wants to be rewarded. The goal is to encourage even the best performers to accomplish more, and not to have them lose their ambition once they have received an incentive.

Designing appropriate incentive programs is a complex business (Van Tiem, Moseley, & Dessinger, 2001). Further, use of pay-for-performance motivators is not always the answer, as incentives go beyond financial rewards. The savvy coach tunes in to what drives each performer to achieve great things and uses that knowledge to supplement any enterprise-sponsored incentive plan.

Metrics

Having a strong management commitment and having the ability to incentivize team members to achieve results are important tools for every coach. Perhaps the most valuable tool a coach can have is performance data and information (metrics). *It is essential to measure whatever nonnegotiable coaching and performance standards and production goals are set for individuals and teams.* Performance information needs to be readily available to coaches and their charges at all times. Regardless of the form, whether hard copy reports, electronic access, or otherwise, this data becomes the focal point for future coaching interactions.

Table 1 shows recommended frequencies for specific types of coaching sessions. By comparing performance data to goals, the coach can easily gauge the accomplishments of individuals and work teams. Where performance is adequate or exceeds goals, coaches seek out causes for the success and develop action plans to replicate the accomplishment across other categories where performance has fallen short. Where performance gaps exist, coaches identify barriers to success and seek solutions to eliminate them. Regardless, without performance tracking data, coaching efforts are fruitless.

Communication

Coaching interactions are dependent on the ability to interpret and distribute useful and productive information. An argument could be made that coaching is all about communication. From the announcement of nonnegotiable performance standards through training and ongoing measurement and tracking, coaching requires the exchange of ideas, the provision of essential information, and a willingness to communicate openly. Clear and accurate communication of performance expectations and results, delivered in a timely and user-friendly fashion, goes a long way toward ensuring success. Communication is also a critical element of the management commitment, incentives, and metrics quadrants.

To be an effective coach, one must possess excellent communication skills, such as active listening and the ability to speak clearly. The ability to interpret others' communication styles and skills is also critical. Often a coach needs to provide instruction on how to relate to others, and the ability to communicate becomes the targeted activity in a coaching session. Clearly, communication is basic to the entire coaching model

Table 1. Coaching Types and Frequency

Coaching Interaction	Description	Frequency
Individual		
Activity Coaching	One-on-one feedback centered around performance activity standards and focused on volume, tactics, and targets of activity. May be done as a team to promote group learning.	Bi-weekly or weekly
Execution Coaching	One-on-one feedback focused on a specific activity to identify barriers that prevent accomplishments and to create an action plan to eliminate them.	Two interactions per month, per direct report
Accomplishment Coaching	One-on-one feedback that looks back at performance and compares it to goals and accomplishments. The purpose is to identify positive trends to replicate and negative trends to eliminate or reverse. Results in an agreed-on action plan to improve performance.	Once per month, per direct report
Team		
Skill/Knowledge Coaching	Work team feedback that follows a set agenda for purposes of group and individual skill and knowledge development.	Once per month
Best-Practice Coaching	Work team feedback session whereby a selected best practice is presented by its owner for purposes of group and individual learning.	Once per month
Accomplishment Coaching	Feedback session centered around work team business results and accomplishments. An opportunity to celebrate successes and debrief ideas on performance improvement.	Once per quarter

and is woven throughout any successful organization. No coaching model could succeed without excellent communication.

Coaching Feedback

Central to the model for achieving business results is coaching itself. As Figure 1 indicates, *coaching feedback* is provided on both an *individual* (one-on-one) and *team* basis. Recall that the first step in defining a coaching model is to establish minimum coaching and performance activity standards. It is through fulfilling these standards that desired business results will be accomplished. It makes sense then, that coaching interactions focus on the level of *activity,* the effective *execution* of these activities, and the *accomplish-*

ment of goals. By examining team effectiveness, the coach is well-positioned to provide valuable feedback on *skills* and *knowledge, best practices,* and *accomplishment.*

Individual

Activity feedback focuses on proactive leading activities, the *execution* of which are *accomplishments.* Accomplishments represent the required tasks and nonnegotiable performance activities that the staff member must complete in order to achieve desired business results. Activity standards must be quantifiable and include a required level and a time frame for completion. The required level of each task or activity has to be sufficient to accomplish the desired business results. Accomplishments, and the activities that lead to them, need to be encouraged, measured, tracked, and reported. Through such measurement, the coach is well-equipped to conduct an activity feedback session. Activity levels should be discussed with direct reports at least every other week, which makes it more likely that they will achieve expected results.

Activity feedback sessions are nonnegotiable for the coach. The interactions can be done individually or as a team, but each individual's accomplishments must be addressed weekly or bi-weekly. Conducting activity level coaching in a team setting promotes group learning and greater accountability. During the discussion, the coach must hold each staff member accountable to the minimum activity standards and make suggestions for improved performance.

Execution feedback sessions narrow the focus to a specific activity. Quite often they arise from an activity feedback session during which a coach notes that the lack of execution of a specific activity is a barrier to accomplishment. A coach then has a one-on-one discussion with a direct report about how to execute a specific task, assignment, or activity more effectively. Skill practices or role plays are often done during these sessions.

Execution feedback is done as opportunities for it arise. Coaches are required to provide a certain amount of this type of feedback as a nonnegotiable coaching activity standard. Generally, coaches should conduct a minimum of two execution feedback sessions per direct report per month. In the case of senior or executive managers, their execution feedback sessions might take on the form of field coaching or listening in on their direct reports as they conduct their own coaching interactions.

The greatest leverage from coaching comes from feedback on accomplishments (synonymous with desired business results). *Accomplishment feedback* sessions take a look back at accomplishments for purposes of identifying positive and negative trends. At least once each month a coach is required to have a one-on-one discussion with each direct report about his or her performance against goals. Using measurement and tracking data, the coach begins the discussion by celebrating when the staff member has performed well. Causes for the accomplishments are explored and discussed, and suggestions are made for how the activities that led to the accomplishment might be replicated in areas where performance is falling short. The same process is followed for areas where the employee is behind plan. Causes for the performance gap are discussed, and ways to increase performance are suggested. The result of the discussion is an agreed-on action plan. The coach holds the staff member accountable for implementing the suggestions over the course of the next month. During that time, through activity and execution coaching, the coach keeps the staff member on track and the person is able to make any necessary adjustments.

Accomplishment feedback is extremely valuable because it is based on hard data that clearly indicate performance against standards and goals. Unlike activity feedback, the focus is backward. During these interactions, the staff member assesses his or her own successes and challenges. Staff members should always express their opinions first, explaining to the coach where and why they feel successful and where and why they are having difficulty. Then the coach can provide input and suggestions to arrive at the final action plan. This method promotes buy-in from the staff member.

Accomplishment feedback should be positioned as a proactive, supportive approach to staff member development. It provides opportunities to identify performance trends over a given period of time. Because these sessions are held monthly, they allow an easy transition into the annual performance review, where there should be no surprises.

Feedback about accomplishments also provides an opportunity to push top performers to even greater heights. Data should be reviewed over time (month-to-month, year-to-year) in preparation for these discussions. In all cases, the coach should identify performance trends, but it is particularly useful for top performers. Having accomplished their goals does not let them off the hook. The goal of the coach is to continue the momentum for positive performance. In the case of the top performer, the action plan is likely to center around increasing the volume of successful activity, allocation of more resources, or providing job aids in order to accomplish even more.

Team

The other type of coaching required is that which addresses an entire work team. Three team-centered types of coaching feedback are *skill/knowledge, best practice,* and *accomplishment.*

First, monthly team meetings should be held to promote *skill and knowledge development.* A standard agenda for these meetings provides a means to measure the development of a specific skill or increased knowledge among the work team. The expected outcome of the meeting is that the accomplishments of the team will improve based on what is learned. Coaches should solicit the active participation of team members. The agenda for such meetings should include:

- A statement of purpose for the meeting that identifies the need to address a specific knowledge or skill gap

- The consequences of not addressing the knowledge or skill gap (lost sales, poor quality, safety hazards, etc.)

- Specific instruction on how to develop the knowledge or skill, including a skill practice opportunity

- A discussion or debriefing period to allow concerns to be addressed and questions to be answered

- An expression of confidence from the coach that team members will practice what they've learned in the session and that performance will improve as a result

The nonnegotiable coaching standard is that the coach will complete one of these sessions on a monthly basis. The nonnegotiable standard for all staff members is that they will attend and actively participate in one of these coaching sessions monthly.

The second type of team coaching interaction involves the identification and presentation of *best practices* from within the team. Each month, coaches have the opportunity to uncover secrets for success, improved processes, and other best practices that are being used by their direct reports. The coach should select one such subject for presentation to the team for purposes of group learning and development. The coach asks the person who demonstrated the best practice to prepare a presentation for the group and assists the staff member by way of an execution coaching session. This results in a *second* monthly team meeting for presentation and discussion of the best practice. In short, coaches hold two monthly team coaching sessions: one to build skills and knowledge, the other to propagate best practices.

Finally, as the model in Figure 1 shows, coaches conduct team coaching sessions related to *accomplishment* on a quarterly basis. Coaches should gather their teams to celebrate successes and highlight individual performances that merit recognition in front of the group. The agenda should also include a reporting of how the business unit is performing against expected results. These review sessions are centered around the measurement and tracking data that should roll up from the individuals to the team. A portion of the meeting should be devoted to debriefing how to replicate successful behaviors and how to overcome challenges and performance barriers.

Summary

Organizations will continue to face fierce competition and pressures to improve performance at an ever-increasing pace. Only yesterday business leaders turned to technology as the answer to keeping up with investor and stakeholder demands. Today businesses are focusing more on performance as the key to achieving results. The power of coaching human capital to greater accomplishment cannot be overlooked. In the end, it is the people who make up an organization who will determine its success. By investing in the development and implementation of a solid coaching practice and inserting it into a well-designed performance system, any organization can experience a substantial increase in business results.

References

Dean, P.J. (Ed.). (1994) *Performance engineering at work.* Batavia, IL: International Board of Standards for Training, Performance and Instruction. As cited in P. Dean (1997), From where begins improvement: Organizational systems and individual performance. In P. Dean and D. Ripley (Eds.), *Performance improvement interventions: Culture and systems change* (pp. 114–137). Silver Spring, MD: International Society for Performance Improvement.

Gilbert, T.F. (1978). *Human competence: Engineering worthy performance.* New York: McGraw-Hill.

Urdang, L. (Ed.). (1985). *The Oxford desk dictionary.* Oxford, England: Oxford University Press.

Van Tiem, D.M., Moseley, J.L., & Dessinger, J.C. (2001). *Performance improvement interventions: Enhancing people, processes, and organizations through performance technology.* Silver Spring, MD: International Society for Performance Improvement.

Stacey L. Gannon *is vice president, sales development, at Citizens Banking Corporation. She manages the sales training and sales performance measurement and tracking functions and is the project manager for the sales process implementation at two banks acquired by Citizens in 1999. Gannon also provides performance consulting and field coaching to management and front-line staff. Since 1981, she has held several sales and sales management positions in the financial services industry.*

Darlene Van Tiem, Ph.D., *is an assistant professor and coordinator of the Adult Instruction and Performance Technology program at the University of Michigan–Dearborn (UM-D). The International Society for Performance Improvement has published two of her books:* Fundamentals of Performance Technology *(2000) and* Performance Improvement Interventions *(2001). Van Tiem spent twelve years in telecommunications and manufacturing as curriculum manager and training director prior to joining UM-D. She has received three prestigious national awards: ISPI 2001 Outstanding Instructional Communication, ASTD Technical Trainer of the Year—1991, and ASTD Outstanding Leadership in the Automobile Industry—1992.*

Life-Centering Stories:
A Powerful Coaching and Self-Discovery Tool
Aviv Shahar

Summary

Life-centering moments concern formative experiences that fashion a template of perception and response that is then active throughout a person's life. Identifying these moments to explore and crystallize their centering quality is a powerful coaching and self-discovery tool. Through the experience of tracing life-centering stories, it is possible to reconnect with one's core strength and discover latent intelligences. The power of life-centering stories becomes magnified by the significance a person may choose to ascribe or re-script to the experience from the perspective of his or her adult choice of vocation and purpose.

In this article, the author describes the theory and application of life-centering stories and offers personal coaching experiences that validate this process as a leadership development tool. Life-centering stories can be customized for use in leadership effectiveness retreats, vision quests, team building, diversity groups, and personal development workshops as well as in one-on-one executive coaching.

The Formative Experience

The early years of life are the most formative. It is a time of explosion of new experience and knowledge every day, every hour, every minute. As the baby explores and expands into new territories, its brain experiences rapid development. Neurons are firing for connections, and new circuitries are connected up with every new step of development. Standing up for the first time, beginning to walk, learning to speak, learning to swim—each of these steps involves expansion into new brain circuitry activation. The engraving-etching power of the early years of experience gradually gives way to an embossing-accumulative type of experience. From ages 12 to 32, the formative experience becomes increasingly more rare and is associated with special meaning or significance.

Template of Response

As each person grows into adulthood, he or she experiences specific moments and situations that carry magnified significance and meaning. Such experiences etch a topographic-like impression that creates a template through which a person will perceive and experience the entirety of his or her life. With life-centering stories, we are interested in unlocking the power and meaning of impressions that were formative of a person's perception and response template.

These experiences can be centered at a point of personal testing or a challenge like having to overcome fear or a difficult obstacle. They could be centered in joy, a sense of liberation, confirmation, or a powerful exchange. The experience can also be ordinary, where the significance of the moment is more subtle and its quality and meaning are hidden. These impressions are like the radium hiding within the pitchblende of life. Exploring life-centering stories is to go into your own Madame Curie lab to tap this material.

The Inside-Out Self-Discovery Nature of Development

An infant lives in a storm of development from the inside out. Everything is new, and the young life is impressionable in the most total way. For the child, everything is big, dramatic, amazing, and thrilling. It is a white canvas on which everything leaves its mark.

Some time later, we begin to learn all the dos and don'ts and the rights and wrongs. We learn what is valued in our environment and how to succeed and be appreciated. It is at this time that the polarity begins to shift from inside-out growth and development to an outside-in accommodation growth. This phenomenon is clearly seen in the following example of two young musicians.

The first learns to play by the classical method of reading music. This first musician does well with the musical score nearby. When the score is taken away, however, a sense of being lost, confused, or paralyzed with doubt governs the experience. The other young musician is given the freedom to explore the instrument and discover the harmonies and scales with the inner ear, where reading music is a secondary aspect. The second musician is not dependent on the external instruction and boundaries of the musical roadmap. The first formative experience with the instrument and the music etched a template of inside-out freedom.

The Expectancy–Reward Mold Withers the Self–Discovery Impetus

Inside-out exploration and experimentation growth expand to satisfy an inner need and propulsion. Outside-in development tends to satisfy the external expectancies such as the need to be accepted and confirmed. It is the difference between the urge and love of discovery and the need to be loved and appreciated. Both are natural urges or needs and play a part in our lives. For most of us as we grow older, we enter the "making it in the world" race and so the second process takes an ever-increasing importance while the self-discovery impulse that was blind to risk in its inception withers away.

How many times while growing up do we get the message, *"In order to succeed in life and in society, you need to . . .,"* whether directly or indirectly?

The Development of the Brain and Self–Discovery

Today we know how critical the process of self-discovery is for the developing brain of a child. A child who discovers a way to perform an action or solve a problem activates in the process a range of brain circuitry function that a child who is merely shown and trained to perform the action will not stimulate. Even when they then both perform the action well, the child who discovered the way to do it brings more of his or her activated self into the process and is therefore more ready and primed to make the next leap of development.

When we do something for the first time, it creates a new synaptic connection. When we repeat the action, it thickens the circuitry. Both processes are fundamental for growth and development. The inside-out discovery process propagates new synaptic connections and triggers latent brain potential. The expectancy-reward pattern tends to accelerate the shift to the thickening process of existing circuitry in a smaller and smaller area.

Life-centering stories are a way to bring back and re-engage more of the activated self. Through telling stories of significant experiences in both youth and later age, we trigger awareness of important inner pathways. These then impart information and understanding about our template of perception and response.

Why We Settle for Less

Self-discovery growth and development is open-ended as it expands from the inside out and has no boundaries. Outside-in development, on the other hand, is already framed within an existing mold. Outside-in learning is propelled by goals and criteria of success as defined outside the person. When the goals have been reached and the rewards have been delivered, the development stops. This is why many of us, even as early as our teens and into adult life, settle for less. It is first-nature for a child to try something again and again in countless ways. Most of us lose this attribute and replace it with doing the minimum work necessary to obtain the desired result. We call it efficiency or productivity, but it is also the narrowing down of possibilities.

Parental and other influences that expedite an early focus on goals and satisfaction as a product outside of oneself cause a person to leave behind untouched the genius locked and latent within. One of the objectives of coaching is to reverse this and facilitate the trigger and release of latent giftedness.

Coaching: The Art of Re-Enlivening and Releasing Arrested Growth

Most people stop or back off from the full explorative and experimental spirit they were once driven by. Society takes it as an unavoidable part of growing up, but it is largely a comfortable, self-fulfilling belief. Who could imagine a society of adults where the majority of people are explorative, creative, challenging the status quo, and daring to try new things every day? We are told this is only for the special few or that we were meant to do that when we were young. Furthermore, when you dare to break the mold, the penalty can be high, so it's better not to try. (The reason for the recent popularity of "reality" shows is because people have backed off from the live spontaneous experimentation of their own lives and are seeking to experience the unchoreographed aspect of living through watching others.)

Growth and development coaching is distinctly different and broader than problem remediation coaching or skill accomplishment coaching. It is focused on facilitating the re-enlivening of the growth patterns that have been stopped or arrested. When people speak of meaningful experiences, whether happy or sad, they touch a living essence that connects them to the self-forming process and releases further potential growth.

The Individualized Nature of Learning and Development

Learning and development is a highly individualized process. We are all unique and do what we do in a unique and individualized way. Your fingerprint is totally unique—there has never been another fingerprint exactly like yours. It is also the case with the unique configuration of your personal traits, qualities, talents, and inclinations. Each person has a unique individualized configuration of aptitude and abilities. In a similar way, how you develop and learn to stand, to walk, to move, to speak, to attract attention and communicate, and the way you learn to perceive the world is uniquely individual.

Effective coaching takes into account the individualized nature of learning and development. It doesn't follow a fixed step-by-step pattern but is the art of customized intervention. The coach must learn to observe, discover, and encourage the unique learning inclinations and growth pattern of the participant.

Developing Along the Permanent Lines of Strength

A child develops naturally along his or her permanent lines of strength. These are the lines of creative tool-making and experimentation leading in adult life to increased competence. The true creators, innovators, discoverers, artists, and leaders of the world are people who have been able to maintain and keep alive the individualized, self-discovery process of inside-out growth and development. They are in touch with a greater part of the activated-self and commune with the significance of their experience and the insight it provides. They follow their unbounded propulsions and talents to enrich their own lives and the world at large.

The essence of coaching leadership development is to facilitate and to help leaders become reconnected with their own unique natural "tool-making" discovery process. Life-centering stories are a coaching tool designed to help rekindle this natural growth process.

The Life–Centering Module: The Lesson of the Tree

The lesson of the tree provides a reflective and meditative reference to one's permanent lines of strength. It highlights the nature of organic growth in which there is a cohesive story line of development. The lesson provides a transformational insight that can be powerful. It is important that the lesson be given with care and encouragement.

If the lesson is provided in a seminar/workshop situation, it is best to conduct it in a natural setting, near a forested area. (If it must be in a classroom, ask people to imagine the picture you describe to them.) Find a tree that has an unusually long branch that stretches out to the sunlight even though it is surrounded by larger trees. Point to the tree and tell the story:

> "It is obvious that the tree struggled to survive its environment. This tree stood in the shade of the larger trees around. It felt the warmth of the sunlight from beyond the other trees, even though it could not experience it directly. It longed to reach the light, for it had within it the knowledge that in the presence of the light it could manifest to its fullest. What the tree did was to concentrate its work and effort and grow a long branch to the side [or high through the other trees] to where it could reach for the sun. The branch grew for a long time in the shade. The tree was propelled by the persistence and the knowledge that as it continued to grow in the same direction it would one day reach the light. It made sure its

roots and trunk continued to support and distribute nourishment to the branch. The outcome was the delight of the branch reaching the light and thereby giving the entire tree further growth and continuance."

Draw a circle in the soil in the shade and another in the light (in a classroom draw the two circles on the board/chart) and explain:

"We humans, unlike the tree, often want to find a shortcut from the shade to the light. We seem at times to not have the patience and perseverance to grow organically to the light, even though in the final analysis it is the only way. We stand in the shade (the first circle) and see the light somewhere else, say in another place or with another person (the second circle). We then try to jump, skip, or fly from the shade to the light. We may want to be exactly like another person, not comprehending that he or she is a compound result of a particular growth pattern and effort. In most cases the shortcut doesn't work. On the rare occasion when it does and the person manages to get to the light, he or she is disoriented, unbalanced, or weakened, having cut him- or herself off from the roots of his or her own organic lines of strength. Exploring life-centering stories is a process designed to reconnect and re-tissue the permanent lines of strength that travel through the high and low points of your life and constitute the cohesive story lines of value, growth, and opportunity."

Life-Centering Stories

There are many ways to work with life-centering stories. It can be done as a personal exercise through journaling, in pairs with a storyteller and a listener, in a trio with a storyteller and two listeners, in a small group, or in a circle.

A Name for the Story

It is a good idea to ask a person to give a name to his or her story. In this way the person centers his or her mind in the essence of the story. The name can be a word or a sentence that captures the value, moral, or significance of the story, for example, "The Spirit of Defiance Awakens."

When the storyteller tells the story for the first time, as is often the case in a workshop, he may not know yet what life-centering value or essence the story holds for the group. Telling the story can become the live harvesting of the value. The name may appear through or after telling of the story. The confirmation and affirmation that telling the story bring offers the opportunity to find or re-script its meaning.

Instructions for Telling a Life-Centering Story

Tell the participants the following:

> "We are going to explore life-centering stories in [pairs/trios/small groups/a circle]. These are stories of moments/situations from childhood through your adult life that have had a life-centering quality.
>
> "There are no right or wrong stories, good or bad stories. There is simply the story you tell and the meaning you are able to find in it or choose to re-script to it.
>
> "Begin by taking a few moments to think of a centering experience you want to tell. Give the story a name. It doesn't have to be the final name; you can later, or through the telling of the story, give it a new or an additional name. Tell the story in details. Describe what you were doing, how you felt, what you thought. Think about the significance this experience had for you and how it impacted you and shaped your perception and character. At the end of the story, try to crystallize the value you harvested from this experience."

Listening to Life-Centering Stories

Coaching the art of listening is an important part of exploring life-centering stories. Taking time to explain, practice, and coach "powerful listening" or "listening with presence" in preparation to telling stories is vital.

Say the following to the listeners:

> "Listen to the story with your full presence. Encourage the storyteller, but don't intervene. Listening to a life-centering story is not interviewing.
>
> "When the storyteller finishes the story, ask if you can offer an additional name to the story. By offering the name of the quality, value, or meaning you found in the story, you can give back the added value you received through listening to the storyteller."

Two Examples of Life-Centering Stories

The Spirit of Defiance Awakens: A Life-Centering Story by Aviv

"It was a rainy winter day and my father and I were on the way to visit a heart specialist. My eighth birthday was still a few months away when our family doctor said that I had a heart condition that needed examination.

"When we entered the crowded hospital, there was very little reassurance. The murky green walls (at the time they didn't know the importance of light colors in hospitals) gave a foreboding background to the many anxious people waiting in the corridors.

"I remember how scared I was when we entered the room to see the heart specialist. I was asked to take off my shirt because they needed to stick on my chest a bunch of things to listen to my heart. The doctor gave me very little attention or comfort (communicating with children wasn't yet an important part of the behavioral paradigm of being a doctor). I remember how worried I was because I was shivering from the cold and in my child-mind I thought things were going to look even worse on the machines reading my heart.

"I tried to calm myself, to take control of my shaking, but standing in front of these cold machines felt lonely and frightening. No words were spoken as we anxiously waited to hear the results. Finally the doctor spoke to my father, not addressing me or even making eye contact with me. In my child-mind that was even more ominous; perhaps I was already dying? 'Your son has a heart condition. It is not threatening, but he needs to be monitored and supervised. He is not to exert himself or to undertake extraneous sport activity and I will need to see him again.'

"More than anything, I loved to swim and run. The doctor's words came across to my child-mind as a death verdict to all I cared for. Waiting for the bus to arrive, my father offered me a sandwich he had prepared. It was the saddest lunch I ever had, but there was something comforting about the love that offered the sandwich.

"Looking through the bus window on the way home, I watched the rain fall on the beautiful orchards and fields. Perhaps something was crying for me because, while it was raining outside, it was also raining inside me.

"Then, while staring at the rain, I felt something welling up inside me. It was the first time I experienced a feeling I would come to know and recognize later in life again. A great internal intensity was building and rising inside me. Although I did not know the words for it, a spirit of defiance was awakened and I turned to my father and said: 'You do know this will not be, I will run, I will run free . . .'

"Whether it was wisdom or instinct, my father listened and made no objections. He probably felt the vulnerability of the moment and thought to keep the discussions for later.

"In the weeks following this occurrence, I took up swimming and running more than ever before. The following year, I discovered the enthralling power of long distance running. I began practicing in earnest and I now know that I was charting my own destiny. I was not going to have the heart specialist deciding my future for me. My resolve and my determination would set me to do and to be and to run free.

"It would take several more years to play out, but my resolve and focus led me to become the youth long distance running champion for Israel. The secret only I knew was that, while I was racing the other runners, I was also racing something else, for it had become a theater in which I was defying the odds against me.

"When we came to visit the heart specialist again, I was not the frightened boy from before. 'Your heart is fine, young man,' he said. I smiled and said, 'I know.'

"This was years before the mind-body connection and its healing power would come to be a part of mainstream conversation. But I now know that this doctor gave me a gift, for his message and demeanor taught me a lesson of defiance and brought me to know a part of myself that was concealed within, waiting to be awakened. It is a part I now know exists in all people, even if dormant, waiting to be released and liberated.

"The spirit of defiance that will not settle to oppression, will rise to make a change, to heal and to bring hope.

"Today as I lead and coach others, my core conviction and passion is to encourage them as leaders to discover the spirit within them and to rekindle their authentic sense of who and what they are and can grow to become.

"This is my life-centering story and the template it etched, enhanced by the meaning I have chosen to bring to it, which empowers my personal mission."

The second example is a story told by a participant in a workshop.

The Value of Showing Up: A Life-Centering Story by Carla

"When my mother was not yet 20 years old, she and my father moved away from their family and friends so that my father would be able to find work. At the age of three, I had a brother who was two and twin sisters who were only nine months old. There was never enough money and my mother finally decided that she too would need to find a job. It was 1954 and there weren't many jobs to be had, especially for a woman who hadn't finished high school. She arranged for someone to take care of us and she left very early in the morning with her paper sack lunch and took a bus to a large manufacturing facility at the edge of town. She walked into the personnel office and asked if there were any positions available. The receptionist said, no, they weren't hiring at that time. My mother went to the bench at the wall and sat down. The receptionist watched her for a while and then said, 'I'm sorry. Maybe you didn't understand. We don't have any openings at this time.'

"My mother replied, 'That's okay. If you don't mind I'll just sit here until you do have an opening.' The receptionist went to find a manager to deal with this unusual applicant. The manager came up to my mother, sat down beside her and said, 'I'm sorry but we're really not hiring at this time.' My mother said, 'That's okay. I'm willing, ready, and able to work. You don't know this about me yet, but I will always be on time, I will give you a full day's work, and you will never be sorry you hired me.' The manager shook his head, told the receptionist to just let my mother sit there, and went away. At 4 o'clock the receptionist began to pack up her desk, and my mother left the office at the same time as the other workers.

"The next day, my mother was waiting at the front door when the manager was unlocking it for the first shift. He ignored her and said hello to several others as they walked in through the front door. My mother took her place on the bench and throughout the day several people came into the office and looked at her as though they weren't quite sure what was happening. At 4 o'clock, the manager came out of his office, handed my mother an application, and said, 'Come back tomorrow ready to work. You've proved your point.' My mother worked at this company for twenty years and then replaced the man who hired her for ten more years.

"My mother told me this story when I was eight years old. I had tried out for the school play and didn't get the part I wanted. Her advice to me then and for many other difficult times was to just show up. Make sure you are there, show that you are ready to participate and that you don't mind if they aren't willing to take you in. I went the same day to the rehearsal for the play and walked up to the director and said, 'I'm here to help in whatever way you need. I will paint scenery, run the sound effects, help the others memorize their lines. I just want to be part of this play.' She was delighted, and I was true to my word.

"Many years later, I was applying for a job for which I was very overqualified. There was a lot of resistance to hiring me, but I needed that job. I told my mother's story to the woman who interviewed me; she laughed and said, 'I'll hire you on the basis of the story.' She hired me, and I stayed with the company for twenty years and left as a manager. The combination of my mother's story and the added strength of my own experiences instructed me many times over the years. It was her story that became part of my story, and its value for me continues to grow and to nourish both self-reliance and belief. As I meet the challenges and obstacles of my life, it is this story that rallies my strength and allows me to meet or defy the expectations of others. I know that showing up speaks louder than any words."

Aviv Shahar *is president of Amber Network (www.ambercoaching.com), a leadership coaching and consulting firm. He coaches a variety of international companies and nonprofit organizations in the areas of leadership development, executive effectiveness, creative thinking, team dynamics, and stress management. He brings twenty years of experience in management and holistic education, philosophy, and spirituality, which he synthesizes into the Whole Person Development methodology in his seminars and public workshops. Prior to this, he was a fighter pilot in the Israeli Air Force.*

Positioning to Create Customer Value Through the Systems Thinking Approach^{SM}

Stephen G. Haines

Summary

This article teaches students of management what positioning is and how to achieve and maintain it to create value in the eyes of the customer. This concept is relatively unknown, but is the key to integrating change in an organized fashion.

History of Providing Customer Value

From order taking, to zero defects, to Deming, to reengineering, the history of providing customer value has evolved over the past twenty years. First, during the Industrial Era, mass production and mass marketing produced products for the "average" customer. This created "order taking" behaviors. Customers selected from what was available. In the 1970s, quality control and "zero defects" were watchwords to refine this internally oriented process even more. In the 1980s, many of the methods made popular in Japan came to the United States (Deming, Juran, PDCA, JIT, Kaizen, and so on).

In the 1990s, cost-cutting, waste elimination, and reengineering were responses to cutthroat global competition. Despite their positive aspects, these efforts are still separate and fragmented solutions. Most firms in the 21st Century still do not have regular and systematic customer feedback mechanisms, so they don't really know what their customers value and are thus unable to respond appropriately. Positioning can help.

Positioning to Create Customer Value

Positioning to create customer value is a simple three-step process. Step 1 is a holistic, intensive focus on customers' wants and needs now and in the future. These wants and needs must become the vision and driving force for your whole organization.

Step 2 is simply to implement the needed changes with a passion for "watertight integrity" to keep all the parts fitting together.

Step 3 consists of radically and strategically redesigning and realigning the entire spectrum of one's business design, processes, and competencies to create customer value. It also means redesigning the fundamental support and capacity-building components of employees and of collective leadership to better fit, integrate, and be attuned with the vision. This step is best depicted by the "Business Excellence Architecture" hexagon model (see Figure 1) beginning with Module 2, Reinventing Strategic Planning.

Module 2: Reinventing Strategic Planning and Positioning

Positioning for value is in the eyes of the beholder. It is defined as what customers perceive they receive from choosing and using a company's products and services in relationship to the "total cost" (financial, psychological, environmental, and otherwise) of doing business with that company instead of with its competitors.

In systems terms, positioning is the "output" customers receive in return for giving their "inputs." It is the multiple outcomes they desire from the range of five World Class Star results (see Figure 2).

Due to advances in information technology and telecommunications, customer value has rapidly evolved from mass production/distribution for the average customer to selling customized relationships and solutions to individual needs and problems. Customer value comes any time and anywhere the customer wants, not when and where the supplier wants.

Customers want relationships with vendors and want to be treated as individuals. Individual customer loyalty matters, not market share. Economy of scope and organizing for the customer become important to a business, not economy of scale and organizing for efficiency. Collaboration and intimacy with customers is *essential*, rather than superficial occasional sales contacts. Customers want responsiveness to their needs and convenience.

Is the Customer King?

There is still a significant gap between attitudes and actions. Although many organizations may say, "The customer is king," according to an extensive survey conducted

The Systems Thinking Approach^SM to Creating Your Competitive Business Advantage

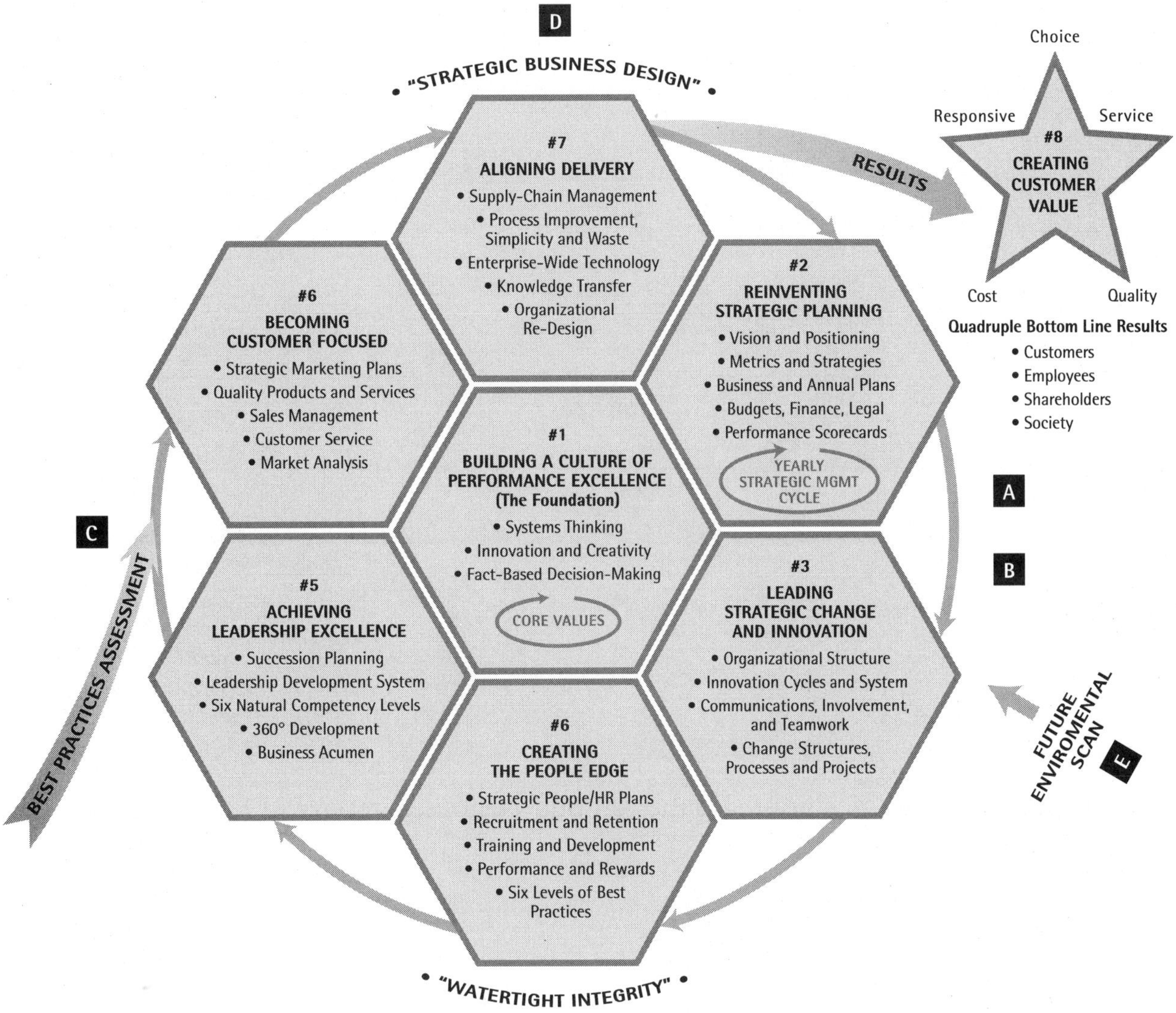

Figure 1. Business Excellence Architecture

by Rath & Strong, a management-consulting firm based in Lexington, Massachusetts, most companies do not live by that credo.

The survey asked more than one thousand managers of Fortune 500 companies how customer-centered their organizations were. While 87 percent of the respondents said delivering value to customers was critical to success, 70 percent also admitted that their performance was driven more by internal operating measures than by external ones. And 80 percent said compensation for employees was not tied to a defined measure of customer satisfaction. The results show that, while most companies are thinking and talking a lot about customer value, there is still a significant gap between talk and action.

Your Competitive Business Edge—Creating Customer Value

C = Personal Choice
Fashion, Control, Self, Customized,
Tailored, Variety, Individuality, My/Me,
Comprehensive Choices, Mass Customization

R = Responsiveness
Fast Delivery, Convenience, Methods,
Timing, Distribution, Flexibility, Access,
Ease of Doing Business, Support Services,
Cooperation

S = Caring Service
Personal Service, Values, Feeling Important,
Customer Relationships, Respect, Caring,
Emotions, Recovery Strategy, Integrity, Empathy,
Sensitivity, Familiar, Trust, Cultural

Customer

Service

**Creating
Customer
Value**

T = Total Cost
Psychological Cost, Price,
Life Cycle, Risk, Opportunity Costs,
Waste/Environment,
Working Conditions,
Product/Service Costs

**Q = High Quality
(Products & Services)**
Features, Authentic, Simplicity,
Information, Technology, Accuracy,
Knowledge, Performance, Reliability,
Functional, Durability, Uses,
Consistency, Stability, Soundness,
Unique, Experiences, Innovative

$$\text{Brand/Recognition/Positioning} = \text{Perceived Customer Value} = \frac{\text{Outputs}}{\text{Inputs}} = \frac{\text{What I Get}}{\text{What I Must Give}} = \text{Benefits}$$

Figure 2. World Class Star Positioning

Strategic Business Redesign

"Value results from a total effort rather than from one isolated step
in the process."   —Alvin Toffler, *Creating a New Civilization*

Creating customer value requires a flexible systems approach that deals with the total efforts, processes, and people of the entire organization (as TQM purports to do for the quality outcome alone). Only a whole-systems model can guarantee successful implementation through the application of a holistic methodology to produce desired client/customer outcomes. The Business Excellence Architecture Model shown in Figure 1 is the result of comprehensive, best practices research. It is validated by the Baldrige National Quality Award "systems" criteria and by the author's highly successful strategic management results in practice.

Customer value is created by the resources and work of a total organization and its stakeholders (owners, suppliers, employees, customers), which creates a value chain, potentially transforming all resources into achieving the results shown in Figure 2 (personal choice, caring service, high quality products and services, total cost, and responsiveness). The model requires that every organizational element be efficiently aligned and effectively attuned as one system achieving customer value, including strategic plans, operations policies, measures, structures, resources, technology, competencies, and business and human resource processes, as well as leadership at all levels.

The Business Excellence Architecture model can guide you along the journey to creating customer value, starting in whichever module you wish. The key is the relationships, fit, and integration of all eight hexagons. This is where almost all organizations go wrong; they work each module separately (for example, focusing only on leadership excellence or becoming customer focused), using different consultants with different frameworks. Such a piecemeal approach is self-defeating.

On the following pages, we'll review the eight modules of our model.

Module 1: Building a Culture of Performance Excellence

Along with positioning the organization's uniqueness in the marketplace is a need to develop the organization's culture and core values for performance excellence. Module 1 includes a culture of innovation and creativity; language, thought processes, and practical tools of systems thinking; fact-based decision making with good information and analysis; and a set of core values that create this desired culture.

Module 2: Reinventing Strategic Planning

This module was explained earlier in this article.

Module 3: Leading Strategic Change

Overall management of cultural transformation to a customer-focused organization is the focus in this module. This requires flexible, responsive people, participative norms of behavior, and empowered work settings. This change is led by setting up specific change management structures to keep all change tasks on track and prevent behaviors from reverting to old ways.

This transformation involves people and social/emotional attunement through understanding and managing the process of change I call "The Rollercoaster of Change[SM]."

It can be very difficult to manage people letting go of the past while nurturing them in developing the persistence and resiliency required for a transformation. Communication and reinforcement plans are also essential to change individual behavior over time. (Organizational change is a misnomer; organizations change only when people do.)

Excellent teamwork is needed everywhere, including in department and cross-functional teams and on business processes, both internally and externally. The key to success is horizontal cooperation and collaboration to serve the customer, not a vertical hierarchy/bureaucracy. Such horizontal teams work far better if they are initially trained in systems thinking and innovation. In fact, "innovation teams" is the right term!

Module 4: Creating the People Edge

A key approach to customer value is having the "soft" people and support elements strategically "in tune" to achieve ongoing world class star results. Strategic personnel/ HR management practices and the system of people management must be attuned to create this "people edge." This means attracting, hiring, motivating, developing, empowering, rewarding, and retaining all crucial staff.

Module 5: Achieving Leadership Excellence

Leadership and management competencies, skills, and strategic communications practices are needed at all levels to ensure that "star results" are achieved. The management skills of trainer, coach, conflict-resolver, and facilitator are vital, as are the abilities to become passionate advocates for and develop close relationships with the customer.

Leadership is the foundation for everything, and leadership development must be an ongoing priority for the collective management team. The requirement for leadership development is especially acute for the middle and senior executives of the organization. They must be trained in the following:

1. Enhancing self-mastery;

2. Building interpersonal relationships;

3. Facilitating empowered teams;

4. Collaborating across functions;

5. Integrating organizational outcomes; and

6. Developing strategic positioning.

Module 6: Becoming Customer Focused

To become customer focused, an organization must

- Engage in strategic marketing, sales planning, and implementation;

- Provide choices and customization for the customer;

- Deliver quality products and services;

- Give high-quality customer service (sometimes called "legendary"); and

- Keep the total cost for the customer low.

In addition, there is a need for strategic budgeting and resource allocation to support the above. Resources of all types must be allocated to providing value for the customer.

Module 7: Aligning Delivery

The last key to success in creating customer value is to realign the entire delivery system to provide value to the customer. Supply-chain management and knowledge transfer can help here. Such methods include:

- Process improvement—including the "continuous improvement" (or Kaizen) concept;

- Enterprise-wide technology—organizational design, restructuring, and technology tools necessary to make sure all of the organization is supportive in creating customer value;

- Increased simplicity and elimination of waste and bureaucracy; and

- On-time delivery, convenience, speed, and responsiveness to customers.

Module 8: Quadruple Bottom Line Results

Even with everything else in place, without setting the metrics in Module 2 for all four bottom lines (customers, employees, shareholders, and society), you will not know whether the results are adequate. Feedback is the key to this type of organizational learning. It includes feedback—to everyone, on everything. Feedback helps us in discovering our hidden assumptions about others' behaviors and performance (sometimes called "mental models"), as well as learning what they want through individual, group, and organizational benchmarking. Feedback is also essential in daily reflection and education and in constant reinforcement of any desired changes.

How to Create Value for the Top Line

There is a significant problem with focusing exclusively on the bottom line. Reengineering, cost cutting, and flatter organizations are not forward-looking customer strategies, but tools for survival. Lowering costs may bring an improved bottom line in the short run, but often severely damage an organization's long-term viability.

Anyone can cut the bottom line in the short term. Few can create customer value for the top line over the long term while also reducing costs. Positive, customer-focused strategies and product innovation are key sources of building a competitive advantage that can sustain an organization's growth. Only in the hands of truly differentiating leadership can competitive customer-focused strategies be effectively implemented.

The critical steps to creating customer value include:

1. Determine your primary customer.

2. Analyze what your customer values and your ability to deliver it versus our "star results" criteria.

3. Assess what differentiates your organization from your competitors.

4. Estimate the cost of each source of differentiation. Remember that adding features usually increases your cost and/or complexity and that improving quality usually simplifies the organization and reduces cost.

5. Test each source of value for sustainability versus the competition, and define your positioning in the marketplace in the eyes of your customers.

6. Reduce activities or waste that do not affect your chosen positioning.

7. Align and attune your complete strategic business design to this position.

8. Implement, protect, change, and continuously improve your competitive edge through positioning.

How to Start

Option 1: Start with an executive briefing and plan-to-plan event on positioning and strategic business design. This is step 1 of a strategic planning process: "educating" about systems thinking, strategic planning, and customer focus; "organizing" for the actual planning process; and "tailoring" the process to your unique needs.

Option 2: Assess your organization versus the Centre for Strategic Management's Business Excellence Architecture via an online web-based assessment instrument, "The Fast Track to Building on the Baldrige."

Option 3: You can also work through the A-B-C-D-E systems phases as follows:

Phase E—Environmental Scan.   Conduct environmental scanning and market research to clarify your customer's wants and needs versus "star results."

Phase A—The Ideal Future Vision.   Set up the planning or strategic change leadership steering committee as well as the rest of the crucial processes and infrastructures for success in strategic management (planning and change). Make creating customer value a major strategy and change project. Clarify your vision and values around this.

Phase B—Measures of Success.   Determine your goals and their measures of success using the five "star results" and quadruple bottom line categories.

Phase C—Strategic Business Redesign Using the Business Excellence Architecture Model.   Conduct a complete strategic business assessment and redesign of the total organization by doing the following:

- Assess your organization versus the Centre's Business Excellence Architecture model online (as shown above);

- Map the key processes. Identify and eliminate the waste by setting up a "simplicity police team";

- Set up core strategies as the primary means to redesign your organization toward your vision of "customer value." Use the eight hexagon modules of the Business Excellence Architecture model as a guide;

- Establish small voluntary innovation and strategy sponsorship teams of executives and managers with a passion for each strategy/module;

- Conduct a plan-to-implement day to kick off the implementation process; and

- Assist in automating and networking processes once they are realigned. Use a technology steering group to coordinate.

Phase D—Implementation and Change.   Begin strategy implementation (and culture change) using the strategy sponsorship teams as the primary vehicles to guide and support creating customer value. However, first:

- Educate the strategy sponsorship teams;

- Assist them in identifying, leading, and carrying out specific activities under each core strategy; and

- Conduct an annual strategic review (and update) each year to formally keep your process fresh and successful.

The key is to just begin!

References

Band, W. (1991). *Creating value for customers: Designing and implementing a total corporate strategy.* New York: John Wiley & Sons.

Collins, J.C., & Porras, J.I. (1997). *Built to last: Successful habits of visionary companies.* New York: HarperCollins.

Crosby, P.B. (1992). *Quality is free.* Denver, CO: Mentor Books.

Deming, W.E. (1990, November 15). *USA Today.*

Drucker, P. (2002). *Managing in the next society.* New York: St. Martin's Press.

Haines, S.G. (2000). *Systems thinking approach to strategic planning and management.* Delray Beach, FL: CRC Press.

Hamel, G., & Prahalad, C.K. (1994). *Competing for the future.* Boston, MA: Harvard Business School Press.

Hope, T., & Hope, J. (1998). *Competing in the third wave.* Boston, MA: Harvard Business School Press.

Juran, J.M. (Ed.). (1998). *Juran's quality handbook* (5th ed.). New York: McGraw-Hill.

McTaggart, J.M., Kontes, P.W., & Mankins, M. (1994). *The value imperative: Managing for superior shareholder returns.* New York: The Free Press.

Mintzberg, H., Ahlstrand, B., & Lampel, J. (1998). *Strategy safari: A guided tour through the wilds of strategic management.* New York: The Free Press.

Peppers, D. & Rogers, M. (1997). *The one to one future: Building relationships one customer at a time.* New York: Doubleday.

Rath & Strong, Inc. (2000). *Six sigma pocket guide.* Lexington, MA: Author.

Ries, A., & Trout, J. (2001). *Positioning: The battle for your mind* (20th ed.). New York: McGraw-Hill.

Toffler, A. (1995). *Creating a new civilization.* Atlanta, GA: Turner Publishing.

Treacy, M.J., & Wiersema, F. (1995). *The discipline of market leaders.* Reading, MA: Addison-Wesley.

Trout, J., with Rivkin, S. (1996). *The new positioning.* New York: McGraw-Hill.

Vaghefi, M., & Huellmantel, A. (1998). *Strategic management for the 21st century.* Del Ray Beach, FL: St. Lucie Press.

Stephen G. Haines *is a CEO, entrepreneur, and strategist. As a premier systems thinker, facilitator, and pro-lific author, he has over twenty-five years of working closely with over two hundred CEOs. He is a U.S. Naval Academy graduate, has a master's degree in OD from George Washington University, and has completed doc-toral work in educational psychology from Temple University in Philadelphia. He is president and founder of both the Centre for Strategic Management and Systems Thinking Press. He was previously president and part owner of University Associates.*

Organizational Success Through Collaborative Consulting

Neil J. Simon and James E. Agnew

Summary

The success of today's enterprise and its long-term viability are dependent on the accurate definition and assessment of new challenges, alignment and integration of the organization's vision and strategies by the leadership, and the cohesiveness and dedication of committed stakeholders.

This article presents a collaborative process for helping your organization create a remarkable future by helping people formulate innovative business strategies and unleashing their potential to achieve it.

Introduction

Today's tumultuous environment has created new business, leadership, and employee needs. There are several factors influencing the development of "new ways" of doing business in what the authors refer to as the "new normal." Today's business is constantly being disrupted by significant changes in the economic climate (for example, worldwide stock markets' rise and fall, economic business scandals) that have a direct impact on daily operations of business. Businesses are being "right sized," merged, and acquired, as well as reorganized, creating continual churning and uncertainly in the business. The business design for today's organizations is one of dynamism and fluidity, while at the same time able to respond to the continual changes thrust on business.

New factors have come into play for American organizations around national security. Maslow's assumptions of safety and security have been re-verified since the events of 9/11/01. Individual workers, their families, and their organizations have had to address new and real fears that have impacted the effectiveness and efficiencies of business, creating additional anxieties and concerns.

Twenty-first Century leadership is experiencing a change in historic patterns. We have seen significant changes in the last decade in issues of mutual loyalty (the organization taking care of the employee and the employee taking care of the organization). Additionally, we have gone from a pattern of having one to two employers in a lifetime career to one of as many as five to seven employers over the course of a lifetime.

The above factors have impacted workers a great deal, leading them to believe that their skills and contributions are a negotiable commodity, frequently referred to as "intellectual capital." Workers have redefined the concept of professional success. Rather than their worth being based on acknowledgment from the organization for their work contributions (promotion, salary, and bonus), workers now seek personal achievement and fulfillment. Businesses are now shifting their strategies to reflect this shift in worker thinking, offering such incentives/rewards as increased personal time, opportunities for telecommuting, and so on. As organizations deal with the changing factors, they strive to harness intellectual capital for sustainability, profitability, and growth.

Fundamental Business Elements

An organization's profitability, growth, and sustainability are driven by the alignment of five fundamental business elements:

- Vision

- Mission

- Guiding values or principles

- Strategic planning

- Business planning

The *vision* of an organization is its expressed "picture" of the future state (ten years and beyond). It is a description of the desired future that an organization attempts to realize. It is expressed as a dream or a description of an ideal state. This vision, if adopted by the organizational members, becomes the common aspiration for employees and decision-making driver for the organization.

The *mission/purpose* is the organization's fundamental reason for existence. It is "how" the organizational members are expected to fulfill the vision. It states the specific duty or services or purposes that the organization has imposed on itself. A mission often reflects the core values of the organization and expresses what the organization "is about."

The *guiding values or principles* of the organization reflect the expectations that the organization has for member behavior as they accomplish their work. Principles and values are the written and unwritten "rules" (norms and mores) that guide the development of the organization's culture.

The *strategic plan* is the chosen direction that the organization will follow to fulfill the mission and vision and the associated measurables (what will be measured to see whether success has been achieved). The plan focuses on "how" the organization will achieve the vision and mission, incorporating the guiding values or principles. The strategic plan encompasses a three- to five-year horizon.

The *business plan* is the specific means by which an organization intends to pursue its goals and objectives. It is the annual course of action that the organization and its membership will take to do the work. The parts of the organization contribute components to the business plan, such as the financial plan, marketing plan, operations plan, and human resource plan. These annual business plans are developed to support the strategic plan and interlock with each other over the period of the strategic plan. The business plan is also the basic plan used to develop division, group, and individual employee performance plans. These are adjusted annually based on the internal and external business and performance factors.

If all these elements are not aligned, the organization loses critical time, resources, intellectual capital, and competitive advantage, which in today's fast-moving workplace can mean rapid death or dissolution of stakeholder commitment.

Based on the complexities of organizations and the conditions imposed by the new normal environment, traditional methods (authoritarian, autocratic, laissez faire) of achieving success are no longer viable. The strategy we have found most commonly employed with the best results today is called collaboration.

General Definition of Collaborative Consulting

Collaborative consulting is a preemptive means by which an organization achieves alignment of the business elements, resulting in strategic and personal success through stakeholder commitment. It is a highly interactive way of considering the individual's knowledge, opinions, and experiences in the formulation of organizational strategies and directions, all of which benefit the organization as a whole.

Overview of the Collaborative Consulting Phases

The authors' specific collaborative consulting process, the A^2D^4 Collaborative Process, consists of six phases. (This process was described in a previous article published in an earlier *Annual* [Simon, 1998]. For a more detailed description of the process,

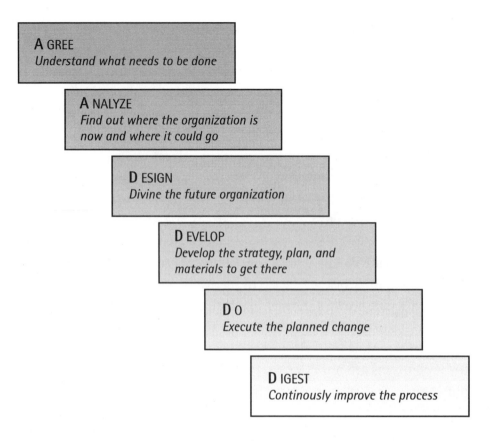

Figure 1. An Overview of the Collaborative Consulting Process

please refer to the original article.) An overview of the phases of the process can be seen in Figure 1.

Each phase has specific collaborative goals and deliverables that assist in the continual alignment of the organizational elements. Each phase is characterized by a cross-functional team that is representative of the organization as a whole. New teams are created for each phase, with select members remaining from previous phases to ensure alignment, continuity, and feedback.

The first phase, the Agree Phase, addresses leadership issues by creating a common understanding of leadership challenges and determining what work has to be accomplished. In every organization, different leadership groups perceive differences in the work that needs to be done as well as the degree and extent of any problems. Examples of leadership groups include unions, executive management, and department or division management, such as marketing, finance, and operations.

It is obvious that union and management leaders have different goals based on the constituency each represents. Each leader having different perceptions based on his or her background and perspective creates a natural conflict of objectives. This conflict opens the door for the initial intervention in the collaborative process.

A collaborative approach is utilized to achieve a win/win scenario. Once that win/win scenario has been defined, a "commission contract" is created and signed by all leadership parties. This results in sponsorship committed to assembling key leaders throughout the organization and communicating what needs to be done. This critical agreement must come from the "top of the house" to ensure that leadership commitment is visible to all stakeholders.

Once an agreement is achieved, an Analysis is conducted by a cross-functional team representative of the organization. The job of the analysis team is to conduct three types of analysis. The first is an internal study of the organization, exploring the organizational structure and processes that are creating the prevailing environment. A second analysis, a benchmark study, is conducted to determine the "best in class" organization that has succeeded in the challenged area. The third analysis is a gap analysis that determines, by reviewing the data collected in the previous two analyses, the gap between where the organization is and where it needs to go.

The Design Phase creates the structure for a solution that fits the organization. Each organization is unique in that it has a specific constituent structure defined/maintained by its organizational culture. The design team utilizes the data from the previous phases to create a solution design that has the highest probability of membership acceptance and approval.

The design team responsibilities include obtaining input from each segment of the organization and the creation of relationships with significant stakeholders with respect to organizational strategies.

The Development Phase focuses on the creation of a plan for how the solution will be implemented throughout the organization. This phase includes such elements as leadership roles and responsibilities, timing, feedback mechanisms, transition materials, and communication mechanisms.

The Do Phase is the execution and implementation of the results of the Development Phase. Coaching of leaders in order to enhance their collaborative skills is accentuated during this phase.

The final phase, the Digest Phase, is another ongoing collaborative process that focuses on the evaluation and continual improvement of the plan.

Collaborative Consulting Success Measures

The actual collaborative consulting success measures are established during the Agree Phase for the entire process. Each phase also has its unique sets of success measures. (See Table 2 for some sample success measures.) The A^2D^4 Collaboration Consulting Process meets the following critical criteria for success:

Intervention Effectiveness.   The result of any intervention must fit the organizational culture. Each organization has a basic structure that is unique to its social system and that must be honored. It is important to recognize that transplanted "canned" programs or solutions are rarely successful in the long term. The Collaborative Consulting Process incorporates the organization's social system in the development of its solution.

Stakeholder Support.   The collaborative activities must be inclusive, soliciting input from the entire organization. This creates an "I am important" mentality resulting in organizational commitment for its win/win benefits. In other words, based on the individual feeling important, he or she contributes knowledge, skills, and opinions to the workplace that merit consideration and satisfy personal goals through organizational success.

Improved Business Results.   Collaborative consulting results in a flexible and responsive structure of the organization, which in turn yields better business results.

Return on Investment/Employee.   Actual benefits of collaborative consulting can be measured both by using traditional financial means as well as by using intellectual capital measures. Table 1 defines the categories of intellectual capital while Table 2 shows the impact of the collaborative process on a variety of organizations.

Conclusion

Sponsor and stakeholder commitment is critical to collaborative success. Without sponsorship from leaders and support from organizational members, any plan is doomed to fail. All stakeholders, however, share a vested interest in achieving success, so this can help to drive their commitment.

Years of experience with this process show that, in addition to the *financial benefits,* some of the more sustaining attributes of collaborative consulting are *culture sensitivity*—creating a process that fits the organization; *inclusiveness*—garnering input from the entire organization; and *increased effectiveness*—generating stakeholder commitment.

Reference

Simon, N. (1998). The A^2D^4 process for designing and improving organizational processes. In *The 1998 annual: Volume 2, consulting* (pp. 219–236). San Francisco, CA: Pfeiffer.

Table 1. Definitions of Intellectual Capital

	Intellectual Capital (Forms of Knowledge) *Discovering, collecting, and sharing the organization's knowledge for the purpose of increasing competitive advantage.*				
	Human Capital	**Structural/ Physical Capital**	**Relational/ Collaborative Capital**	**Social Capital**	**Competitive Capital**
Definition	The tacit, nonexplicit knowledge, skills, and experience of the workers.	Structures, systems, and processes people create to operate the firm. How the goods and services are produced.	Workers' relationships with suppliers, with customers, and with the community.	Internal exchanges creating wealth or benefit deriving from social relationships, which produce expectations of returns and creation of community good.	Knowledge derived from team-based analysis of competitors and competitiveness (a specialized form of social capital).
Examples	• Job skills • Capabilities • Education • Training • Experience	• Corporate culture • Human resource information system • Organizational design • Policies and procedures • Capital equipment • Utilization of human resources (mind and body) • Formal and informal internal networks	• The relationships (knowledge about others, information, skills, and/or abilities) people create outside the system • Managing relationships with suppliers, external networks, and regulatory resources	• Interpersonal relationships • Language of the organization • Actions created by personal relationships • Trust	• Specialized knowledge generated by specific employee activities created and sanctioned by the organization • Networks and shadow teams evolved to discover competitive information

Table 2. Impact of Collaborative Consulting

Client Type	Intellectual Capital					Financial Capital
	Human	Structural/ Physical	Relational/ Collaborative	Social	Competitive	
Service Association	Employees cross-trained two or three deep	• Allowed for instantaneous ad hoc problem solution teams • Created robust and flexible structures responsive to consumer and organizational needs • Developed new and standardized processes and procedures	Created collaborative culture			• Increased revenue generation per employee by over $130K • Added over $3 million to gross revenues • Reduced administrative expenses to 30 percent below industry average.
Manufacturing	• Installed team-based work system • Team created its own business plan • Team developed its own business training program	Reduced the need for direct supervision from 1:8 to 1:25	Created collaborative culture Created customer service culture		• Created unique brand identity and positioning • Developed new competitive products • Integrated current product offerings into hybrids	• Team operates at or below budgeted level • Team added significantly to plant bottom line • Achieved 98 percent equipment uptime
Health Care Services Division	Increased workers' knowledge and skills	• Created competitive structure for the new division • Merged nine divisions into one • Developed new standardized processes	Created collaborative culture	Creation of new relationships leading to product cross-selling		• Reduced real estate costs • Reduced computer system costs • Reduced operational costs

Table 2. Impact of Collaborative Consulting, *continued*

Client Type	Intellectual Capital					Financial Capital
	Human	Structural/ Physical	Relational/ Collaborative	Social	Competitive	
Small Service Firm	Cross-training for each role	• Optimized support structure for customer service support and role contribution • Created competitive intelligence system	• Created collaborative culture • Created customer service culture		Created unique positioning	• Increased revenues from $8 million to $12 million • Increased profits 35 percent
Municipal Service	Complete cross-training program	• Removed two levels from hierarchy • Merged three organizations into one • Created new and standardized processes	Created customer service culture			• Reduced workers' comp claims by 35 percent • Increased worker morale 45 percent • Reduced costs 35 percent • Increased profits 15 percent
Emergency Response System	Increased EMT knowledge and skills leading to decrease in community mortality rate	Pioneered new procedures that aided the entire industry	• Created collaborative culture • Created community mutual aid system			Consolidation of expenses through mutual aid system

Neil J. Simon *is the CEO of Business Development Group, based in Ann Arbor, Michigan. He has over thirty years' experience in working with organizations and individuals to improve performance. His work focuses on organization leadership, strategic change, and implementation utilizing his A^2D^4 collaborative consulting approach. He works nationally and internationally with organization to strategize, innovate, design, or re-design processes, departments, divisions, or entire organizations to optimize organizational performance.*

James E. Agnew *is a senior consultant and COO with Business Development Group, Inc. He spent over thirty years as an executive for a Fortune 5 corporation, gaining an extensive background in operations management and strategic planning. He has organized and directed global business units, launched facility expansions, and innovated employee involvement strategies. His expertise in strategic management is further enhanced by advanced studies at Harvard and Duke Universities.*

Change the Snapshot:
Change Perceptions
Marcia Ruben and Jan M. Schmuckler

Summary

Perceptions are clearly important to executives, as they can make or break a career. This article addresses the most frequent questions that executives may ask themselves and their human resources development (HRD) practitioner about perceptions and how to change them. The HRD practitioner may want to bring in an external coach to assist the executive in understanding the potency of the perceptions of others and for help in changing the behaviors that led to any misperceptions. This article also provides case examples from the authors' coaching and consulting practice.

Introduction

Just as a photograph becomes a memory of our perceived reality or an indelible reminder of a particular moment in time, when we first meet and work with people in business, we form a snapshot or first impression. The snapshot is our initial perception of people and may include our conclusions about why they act as they do, the kind of people they are, or their roles. For instance, when we meet new executives who appear poised and confident and seem to be obtaining results, our impression is positive. Quickly we determine that we trust, like, or want to work with them. On the other hand, when we meet leaders whose behaviors are curt and abrupt or who seem to think they know all the answers, we decide that they are arrogant and, perhaps, that we don't like, don't trust, or don't want to work with them. Whether accurate or not, we keep these perceptions filed away in our memories. Perceptions, like snapshots, are difficult to change once they are embedded in a person's mind. The truism that you can't make a first impression twice is particularly powerful in a business setting.

Perceptions have the capability of enhancing or destroying careers. For example, in the political arena, candidates viewed as "stiff," "weak," "dull," "quick to anger," or "not in touch" have found their political ambitions dashed. In the corporate arena, once highly esteemed, high visibility executives have been seen in the public eye as "thieves," "crooks," or unethical. Whether these perceptions were true or not, once they became embedded in the public psyche, these executives' careers were doomed.

In the same way, all people who work in thousands of other business and organizational settings must realize that perceptions others have of them may have the power to either boost or derail their careers. Unfortunately, and all too commonly, negative perceptions are more likely to be unspoken, that is, not directly and clearly articulated to the executive. If executives are not aware of these perceptions and do not take immediate action to change them, their careers could be in jeopardy.

Identifying Common Perceptions That Derail Executives

There are a number of common perceptions that can derail an executive career. The ones that we have found most common in our practice include being perceived as:

- Too aggressive in making changes;

- Not a team player;

- Not influencing the right people;

- Not collaborative enough;

- Arrogant;

- Not on board with the corporate vision;

- Running roughshod over direct reports; and/or

- Playing favorites with direct reports.

One of the most difficult challenges for executives is changing these negative perceptions others have of them, particularly perceptions that have the capacity to impact their careers. Typically, others' impressions are conclusions about an executive's behavior, style, or way of thinking and being.

With the assistance of a neutral third party, such as a coach, executives can become aware of the perceptions or snapshots they are creating and of how these affect their careers. In addition, an HRD practitioner can collaborate with a coach to form a support team for the executive to reinforce new behaviors and ideas. Such a process can make a significant difference for the success of an executive.

Coaching helps executives change the negative perceptions that others form about them because coaches can illuminate blind spots and provide crucial, straightforward, honest feedback.

Commonly Asked Questions

Some questions that executives or HRD practitioners have asked us about this topic follow, along with some examples from our coaching experience.

- Do first impressions really last?

- I know myself. Why can't I trust my self-perception?

- If I'm doing the "right thing" for the company, why should I care about other people's perceptions?

- Do I really have to take others' perceptions seriously?

- How can others help me?

- How will people know that I am trying to change their perceptions of me?

- Do I have to admit that I may have made a mistake?

- Why is rebuilding trust so difficult?

Do First Impressions Really Last?

Because of the nearly indelible nature of perceptions, you will not change them over-night. Changing perceptions takes time. In fact, it usually takes six to nine months. Often people in the organization have to be told of a leader's new behaviors and see them demonstrated over and over again. HRD practitioners can reinforce the changes leaders make with their coaches.

> Josephine, a senior-level executive in a high-technology company, was a fast-rising star. She learned from 360-degree feedback that her direct reports thought that she was taking over their projects and enjoyed solving their problems for them. Their impression was that she did not want to give her staff opportunities for growth and development of new skills. On the other hand, she stayed up late every night, feeling resentful about her staff's seeming inability to take responsibility for their own work. Over the course of many months and by working closely with her coach, she began to understand how her own behavior was contributing to the perceptions; with the help of her HRD practitioner, she began to provide professional development for her staff.

In addition, she became aware of her own micro-management behavior and how it limited her staff's growth. As her team's members began to develop their own skills, Josephine started letting go. Through continued coaching and developmental work, she realized that providing clear direction, trusting her staff, and allowing them to manage their own projects with minimal supervision was a key success factor for all of them.

First impressions can last forever or until the executive works long and hard to change them. When an executive demonstrates automatic or habitual behaviors, these reinforce the belief that peoples' perceptions are correct. In addition, they can lead people to make up their own reasons for why an executive is doing what he or she is doing. In order for others' perceptions to change, they must see the executive doing any new behavior over and over again for long periods of time.

I Know Myself. Why Can't I Trust My Self-Perception?

Research done by Mike Lombardo of Lominger Inc., and reported at the 10th Annual Lominger User's Conference in 2002, indicates that self-reports on 360-degree feedback are usually .75 above actual behavior on a 5-point scale. This means that people typically view themselves much more favorably than others view them. This "self-halo" effect is in part a defense mechanism. In fact, we rarely know how we come across unless we have specifically taken the time and effort to develop self-awareness, both by becoming an objective, third-party observer of our own behavior and by asking for the objective, honest feedback from others whom we trust. Lominger's research (Lombardo, 2002) indicates that people who derail in their careers are most likely to overrate themselves on 360-degree instrumented feedback. "Self" was consistently found to be the least accurate rater, particularly on interpersonal skills. Most successful executives know what they do well, where their skills and performance are mediocre, and, most importantly, what they need to improve. The best way for executives to protect themselves against derailment is to ask for detailed information about strengths and areas for development early enough to compensate for weaknesses.

One way for executives to gain perspective about others' points of view is to conduct a 360-degree feedback process or to cross-check their self views with others outside of their department, division, or organization. Leaders can learn a lot from people with whom they interface at work. It's important to compare self-appraisal with the results of feedback from others, keeping in mind the possibility of errors in self-rating. Then executives can use the information to enhance or change behaviors or perceptions to form a view based on reality.

If I'm Doing the "Right Thing" for the Company,
Why Should I Care About Other People's Perceptions?

> Steve, an executive VP, started on a controversial course of action without communicating his motives and intent to his peers and direct reports. Steve did not think it was necessary to communicate his intentions because he knew he was making the right decisions for the company to succeed and that his intentions were purely honorable. However, Steve was perceived as a "me only" player because he did not share information with his peers or his team, who thought he was overly ambitious and wanted another promotion. Once Steve was viewed in this way, that view became the lens for all future interactions. In other words, Steve's team and his peers formed a snapshot and that snapshot "stuck," even when his behavior and intentions did not match their perception. The only way Steve was able to change the snapshot was by making his intentions explicit with the help of coaching so that he was able to influence the way people thought about him.

Negative perceptions can truly inhibit our ability to succeed. Executives might actually have their company's best interests at heart, but if others do not share that view or see things differently, it does not matter. Having honorable intentions is not enough; executives must make their thinking and their reasoning visible so that others can understand the changes they want to make.

Do I Really Have to Take Others' Perceptions Seriously?

No matter what the reality of the situation is, executives must take others' perceptions seriously. Perceptions about the employment contract of former General Electric CEO Jack Welch, within the context of revelations about greed at the executive level of corporations, threatened to tarnish what had been a stellar reputation. Therefore, he wrote a letter to *The Wall Street Journal* (Welch, 2002) and stated, "One thing I learned during my years as CEO is that perception matters. And in these times when public confidence and trust have been shaken, I've learned the hard way that perception matters more than ever."

Perceptions are not just "shadow puppets," as Michelle, a VP at a biotech firm, told us. Perceptions shape reality.

> At first, it was difficult for Michelle to accept that perceptions of her were important, since Michelle was achieving results for the company at meteoric speed. Unfortunately, Michelle had overlooked her peers while making rapid changes, and they were furious. The company culture was one of collaboration. Her peers saw her behavior as "empire building." Michelle knew that empire building wasn't even on her radar screen, so she dismissed their perceptions and did not take them seriously. After a 360-degree interview process, Michelle was able to understand

why that perception existed. Then she could begin rebuilding her image—changing the snapshots.

Work on changing perceptions is more important than work on changing or separating reality and perceptions. Defensiveness and argument do not change perceptions and often reinforce the perceptions as reality for the other person. The question to ask and reflect on is "How do others see me?"

How Can Others Help Me?

Sean, an executive with a fast-growing high-technology company, had worked for a number of East Coast companies before relocating to the West Coast. The corporate cultures in which he had flourished were aggressive and encouraged long hours with a "pull no punches" type of communication. When Sean received feedback from his boss that his style was rubbing peers and direct reports the wrong way, he enlisted the help of a coach. With the assistance of his coach, Sean created a network of internal people within his department with whom he had built good relationships and included his HRD practitioner. Sean was candid in his desire to change others' perceptions, and he asked these colleagues if they would be of assistance. First, they helped him understand the company culture in terms of acceptable and unacceptable behavior. Next, they advised him about behaviors that were working and, specifically, what was not working. This feedback was invaluable to Sean. Over the course of many months, his colleagues helped Sean create new perceptions about his behaviors. And over the course of many months, Sean learned to adapt to the more laid-back culture.

One of the best ways to deal with others' bad perceptions is to invest time in creating alliances with advocates who can head off time-consuming miscommunications. An alliance of peers, direct reports, HRD practitioners, and one's boss can support new behaviors. These advocates can be a built-in support network that can help to change the perceptions of the rest of the organization. In some companies, it is important to find a mentor or sponsor who can help you understand the culture of the organization and what behaviors are needed to change some of the perceptions that people hold. A side benefit can be that the organization will see the executive as a team player because of his or her working with others.

How Will People Know That I Am Trying to Change Their Perceptions of Me?

An executive, Jane, learned in an "influence" workshop that she did not act like an expert during group meetings. Her peers had an unstated expectation that, because of her functional role and title, Jane was to talk and behave in a certain way. At this workshop, Jane learned that it would not be enough to come to the same group of peers and act like an expert. She had to tell them, "I am the expert in this room, and therefore we need to do X." Without her directly pointing out her new behaviors, the team would have treated her in the same way as they had before the training. They had an initial snapshot of her that did not change just because Jane attended a training class. Their perceptions changed when Jane made explicit her role and her new behavior.

Changing behavior is not enough. Executives have to tell people that they intend to change their behavior and specifically show what they are trying to change. Some people don't recognize the new behaviors, because they still see the first "snapshot" that they took. The executive has to help others develop a new perspective. Typically, others don't even recognize that new behavior is occurring unless they are explicitly told.

Do I Have To Admit That I May Have Made a Mistake?

Successful executives admit that they've erred and try to correct their missteps and thereby their image. It's important to admit mistakes, to be vulnerable, and to ask for help in changing others' perceptions. For some executives, admitting mistakes is one of the most difficult things that they have to do. Tom Ucko (1999), a leadership coach, advises, "Simply tell your associates that, in the spirit of continuous improvement, you've chosen to enhance your leadership skills toward becoming the best leader that you can be. This conveys a powerful message about your integrity and models your commitment to professional growth."

> For example, Josh, a senior-level executive who had recently been promoted into a position with much greater responsibility and scope, received feedback that he was favoring some of the staff over others. This information stunned Josh and he decided to call together his new staff and openly share that development was a priority, not only for him, but also for the entire division. Josh stated that he believed that the best executives were always learning and improving and that one of the things he wanted to work on was creating an egalitarian environment. By admitting that his behavior could have led to certain conclusions, Josh cleared the way for a new spirit of development.

Why Is Rebuilding Trust So Difficult?

Trust is earned. It is not automatically given to everyone who has a vice presidential title. An executive earns trust by keeping commitments and following through on what he or she says. Employees hold executives to their word, and if the words are inconsistent or perceived as dishonest, then trust will usually be eroded.

> Tomasina, a marketing executive in charge of a high-profile company-wide project, said she was committed to the project. However, as business conditions and

priorities changed, Tomasina began to divert the budget and resources to other projects without explaining the business case to her team. They came to the conclusion that Tomasina was not backing them and that their participation on the project would doom their careers in the company. Trust in this executive was broken.

Once trust is broken, it is an uphill battle to rebuild it because, once we form a belief about a person's behavior, we then see all behavior through the lens of that belief. Every nuance is viewed as a possible infraction of the broken trust. In Tomasina's case, after she started diverting budget and resources, her staff construed every word and action as meaning that she was not committed to the original project, whether it was true or not. The team refused to trust her because they saw her actions as reinforcing the perceptions that they had formed of broken trust.

Therefore, it is best not to break trust in the first place, but if it is broken, know that it will take a long time to rebuild with lots of consistent behaviors and actions that show trustworthiness. HRD practitioners and coaches can reinforce this message and can help reward executive behaviors that consistently build trust.

Conclusion

Prior to the advent of digital photography, photographs could never be altered. Now photographs can be changed in an instant, but not so with human behavior. Each of us, over the course of our development as fully functional human beings and professionals, develops a set of values, beliefs, and filters that allow us to make meaning and sense of our world. Perceptions become our reality and are quite difficult to change.

In business, many executive careers have stalled because of the perceptions of upper management, peers, customers, and direct reports. Changing those perceptions is up to the executive. Coaches working with executives who want to change others' perceptions of them must first be certain that the executive understands the impact of the perceptions and is motivated to change. Changing the view others hold requires discipline and focused effort on the part of the executive and a long-term commitment on the part of the company.

In some cases, given the demands of the workplace, the speed of business life, and an environment that is not supportive of development, it is simply too late or not possible to change people's perceptions. In these cases, it is wise for executives to choose to live with the results of the perceptions they have created or to move on. As one friend wisely stated, "We always take ourselves wherever we go."

In working with perceptions, the first challenge for coaches is two-fold. They must convince executives that what is going on in their heads—their intentions—may not have been translated by others as planned. The second challenge is that executives have little influence over the filters of others and must find clear and straightforward ways of communicating and behaving that leave little room for doubt. Internal HRD practitioners can be helpful in these situations by reinforcing the behavioral changes that are made and by pointing out the perceptual shifts that the coach is working on with the executive. Because HRD practitioners are inside the organization system, they can provide the coach with important cultural information that can make or break the perceptions others hold of the executive.

It is possible to change the snapshot, and therefore the perceptions others hold of executives, especially when the external coach teams with the internal HRD practitioner. The leadership coach can open up the blind spots for an executive. The HRD practitioner can make the fabric of the organization visible to the coach and to the executive in order for them to see the necessity for changes to occur. Executives who are aware of their blind spots and the true impact of their behavior on others can and have changed how others perceive them. It is not an easy road, but it is also not an impossible one.

References

Lombardo, M. (2002, June 11–14). *Lominger's continuing research.* Paper presented at the 10th Annual Lominger User Conference, Naples, Florida.

Ucko, T. (1999, Spring). *Working together: Straight talk on leadership and teamwork* (newsletter). Corte Madera, CA.

Welch, J. (2002, September 16). Letter to the Editor. *The Wall Street Journal.*

Marcia Ruben, M.S., *principal of Ruben Consulting Group, is a certified management consultant who helps leaders, teams, and companies achieve high performance. Her firm focuses on organizational change management, executive development, and coaching. She has worked with leaders of Fortune 500 high-technology and financial services companies for over twenty years. She graduated Phi Beta Kappa from the University of California, Berkeley, and received her master's of science degree in counseling from California State University.*

Jan M. Schmuckler, Ph.D., *organizational psychologist and leadership coach, works with executives and managers to achieve outstanding business results. Her more than twenty-five years of experience with leading companies in the high technology, biotechnology, and financial sectors around the world brings unique perspectives for competing more effectively. She is VP of programs for the Professional Coaches and Mentors Association and teaches at John F. Kennedy University's coaching program. She received her Ph.D. in organizational psychology from the Wright Institute.*

Contributors

James E. Agnew
17340 West 12 Mile Road, Suite 102
Southfield, MI 48076
  (248) 552-0821
  fax: (248) 552-1924
  email: Jagnew@busdevgroup.com

Kristin J. Arnold, MBA, CPCM
Quality Process Consultants, Inc.
11304 Megan Drive
Fairfax, VA 22030
  (703) 278-0892
  fax: (703) 278-0891
  email: karnold@qpcteam.com

Michael Bergdahl
Michael Bergdahl Associates
Targeted Performance Solutions
P.O. Box 291
Ingomar, PA 15127-0291
  (412) 635-2638
  fax: (412) 635-0418
  email: mbergdahl@aol.com
  URL: www.michaelbergdahl.com

Joelle Davis Carter
RJC Consulting, LLC
P.O. Box 192
Accokeek, MD 20607
  (202) 550-2647
  fax: (301) 203-3013
  email: rjcrndll@aol.com

Pu-Shih Daniel Chen, M.S.
154 Herlong Drive, #11
Tallahassee, FL 32310
  (850) 575-5732
  fax: (734) 264- 4139
  email: Chen@bibledaniel.com

Stacey L. Gannon
4100 Linden Drive
Midland, MI 48640
  (989) 832-0032
  email: stacey.gannon@cbcf-net.com

Peter R. Garber
Manager, Teamwork Development
PPG Industries, Inc.
One PPG Place
Pittsburgh, PA 15272
  (412) 434-2009

W. Norman Gustafson
7428 North Meridian Avenue
Fresno, CA 93720
  (559) 299-2166 or (559) 875-7121
  fax: (559) 875-8848
  email: wngus@hotmail.com

Stephen G. Haines
Centre for Strategic Management
Systems Thinking Press
1420 Monitor Road
San Diego, CA 92110-1545
  (619) 275-6528
  fax: (619) 275-0324
  email: stephen@csmintl.com
  URL: www.csmintl.com
  URL: www.SystemsThinkingPress.com

Cher Holton, Ph.D.
The Holton Consulting Group, Inc.
4704 Little Falls Drive, Suite 300
Raleigh, NC 27609
  (919) 783-7088 or (800) 336-3940
  fax: (919) 781-2218
  email: cher@holtonconsulting.com

H.B. Karp
Personal Growth Systems
4932 Barn Swallow Drive
Chesapeake, VA 23321
  (757) 488-4144
  fax: (757) 488-4144
  email: pgshank@aol.com

Betsy Kendall
319 Cross Street
Carlisle, MA 01741
  (978) 371-2788
  email: betsykendall@aol.com

Steve Kuper
Innovative Strategies, LLC
10 College Avenue, Suite 126A
Appleton, WI 54914
  (920) 993-4405
  fax: (920) 993-4406

Deborah Spring Laurel
Laurel and Associates, Ltd.
917 Vilas Avenue
Madison, WI 53715
  (608) 255-2010
  fax: (608) 260-2616
  email: dlaurel@ameritech.net

Julia Panke Makela
The Graduate School, USDA
Center for Leadership and Management
600 Maryland Avenue, SW, Suite 330
Washington, DC 20024
  (202) 314-3598
  fax: (202) 479-6813
  email: julia_makela@grad.usda.gov

Rick Maurer
Maurer & Associates
5653 North 8th Street North
Arlington, VA 22205
  (703) 525-7074
  fax: (703) 525-0183
  email: rick@beyondresistance.com

Ira J. Morrow, Ph.D.
Department of Management
The Lubin School of Business
Pace University
1 Pace Plaza
New York, NY 10038
  (212) 346-1846
  email: imorrow@pace.edu

Amy Pawlusiak
19989 Gallahad
Macomb, MI 48044
  (586) 412-0998
  email: pawlusiaka@macomb.edu
  email: pawlusiaka@yahoo.com

Edwina Pio
Faculty of Business
Auckland University of Technology
MER, Level 2
46, Wakefield Street
Auckland 1020
New Zealand
  64-9-917999, ext. 5130
  fax: 64-9-9179884

A. Venkat Raman, Ph.D.
Faculty of Management Studies
University of Delhi South Campus
Benito Juarez Road
New Delhi 110 021
India
  (91-11) 687 5875 / 79
  fax: (91-11)687 3749 / 687 5878
  email: venkat@iic.ac.in

Marcia Ruben, M.S.
Ruben Consulting Group
520 Pacheco Street
San Francisco, CA 94116
  (415) 564-7135
  email: marcia@rubenconsulting.com
  URL: www.rubenconsulting.com

John A. Sample, Ph.D., SPHR
Florida State University
2922 Shamrock South
Tallahassee, FL 32309
  (850) 644-8176
  fax: (850) 644-6401
  email: sample@coe.fsu.edu

Jan Schmuckler, Ph.D.
Jan M. Schmuckler Ph.D. Consultation
3921 Burckhalter Avenue
Oakland, CA 94605
  (510) 562-0626
  email: jan@janconsults.com
  URL: www.janconsults.com

Aviv Shahar
Amber Network
15363 NE 201st Street
Woodinville, WA 98072
  (425) 415-6155
  fax: (425) 415-0664
  email: ambercoaching@aol.com

Neil J. Simon
17340 West 12 Mile Road, Suite 102
Southfield, MI 48076
  (248) 552-0821
  fax: 248-552-1924
  email: NJSimon@busdevgroup.com

Steve Sphar
2870 Third Avenue
Sacramento, CA 95818
  (916) 731-4851
  fax: (916) 739-8057
  email: sphar@pacbell.net

Douglas J. Swiatkowski, M.Ed.
Ford Motor Company
Retailer Education and Training
16800 Executive Plaza Drive,
   Mail Drop 9NE-A
Dearborn, MI 48126
   (313) 390-9907
   email: dswiatkowski@hotmail.com

Darlene Van Tiem, Ph.D.
1310 Kensington Road
Grosse Pointe Park, MI 48230
   (313) 884-4311
   email: dvt@umich.edu

Mardy Wheeler
45 High Street
Natick, MA 01760
   (508) 655-7068
   email: mardyw@attbi.com

Martha C. Yopp, Ed.D.
University of Idaho—Boise Center
Adult & Organizational Learning
Boise, ID 83712
   (208) 364-9918
   email: myopp@uidaho.edu

Contents of the Companion Volume, The 2004 Pfeiffer Annual: Training

Editor's Choice

Inventories, Questionnaires, and Surveys

Articles and Discussion Resources

How to Use the CD-ROM

System Requirements

Windows PC

- 486 or Pentium processor-based personal computer
- Microsoft Windows 95 or Windows NT 3.51 or later
- Minimum RAM: 8 MB for Windows 95 and NT
- Available space on hard drive: 8 MB Windows 95 and NT
- 2X speed CD-ROM drive or faster
- Netscape 4.0 or higher browser or MS Internet Explorer 4.0 or higher
- Microsoft Word 97 or higher

Macintosh

- Macintosh with a 68020 or higher processor or Power Macintosh
- Apple OS version 7.0 or later
- Minimum RAM: 12 MB for Macintosh
- Available space on hard disk: 6MB Macintosh
- 2X speed CD-ROM drive or faster
- Netscape 4.0 or higher browser or MS Internet Explorer 4.0 or higher
- Microsoft Word 98 or higher

NOTE: This CD also requires the free Acrobat Reader. You can download this product using the link below:

http://www.adobe.com/products/acrobat/readstep.html

Getting Started

Insert the CD-ROM into your drive. The CD-ROM will usually launch automatically. If it does not, click on the CD-ROM drive on your computer to launch. You will see an opening page. You can click on this page or wait for it to fade to the Copyright Page. After you click to agree to the terms of the Copyright Page, the Home Page will appear.

Moving Around

Use the buttons at the left of each screen or the text at the bottom of each screen to move among the menu pages. To view a document listed on one of the menu pages, simply click on the name of the document. Use the scrollbar at the right of the screen to scroll up and down each page. To quit a document at any time, click the box at the upper right-hand corner of the screen.

To quit the CD-ROM, you can click the Quit button on the left of each menu page or hit Control-Q if you are a PC user or Command-Q if you are a Mac user.

In Case of Trouble

If you experience difficulty using this CD-ROM, please follow these steps:

1. Make sure your hardware and systems configurations conform to the systems requirements noted under "Systems Requirements" above.

2. Review the installation procedure for your type of hardware and operating system. It is possible to reinstall the software if necessary.

   You may call Pfeiffer Customer Care at (800) 274-4434 between the hours of 8 A.M. and 4 P.M. Eastern Standard Time and ask for Pfeiffer Product Technical Support. You can also get support information and contact Product Technical Support through our website at http://www.wiley.com/techsupport.

3. Please have the following information available:
   - Type of computer and operating system
   - Version of Windows or Mac OS being used
   - Any error messages displayed
   - Complete description of the problem.

   (It is best if you are sitting at your computer when making the call.)

Pfeiffer Publications Guide

This guide is designed to familiarize you with the various types of Pfeiffer publications. The formats section describes the various types of products that we publish; the methodologies section describes the many different ways that content might be provided within a product. We also provide a list of the topic areas in which we publish.

FORMATS

In addition to its extensive book-publishing program, Pfeiffer offers content in an array of formats, from fieldbooks for the practitioner to complete, ready-to-use training packages that support group learning.

FIELDBOOK Designed to provide information and guidance to practitioners in the midst of action. Most fieldbooks are companions to another, sometimes earlier, work, from which its ideas are derived; the fieldbook makes practical what was theoretical in the original text. Fieldbooks can certainly be read from cover to cover. More likely, though, you'll find yourself bouncing around following a particular theme, or dipping in as the mood, and the situation, dictate.

HANDBOOK A contributed volume of work on a single topic, comprising an eclectic mix of ideas, case studies, and best practices sourced by practitioners and experts in the field.

An editor or team of editors usually is appointed to seek out contributors and to evaluate content for relevance to the topic. Think of a handbook not as a ready-to-eat meal, but as a cookbook of ingredients that enables you to create the most fitting experience for the occasion.

RESOURCE Materials designed to support group learning. They come in many forms: a complete, ready-to-use exercise (such as a game); a comprehensive resource on one topic (such as conflict management) containing a variety of methods and approaches; or a collection of like-minded activities (such as icebreakers) on multiple subjects and situations.

TRAINING PACKAGE An entire, ready-to-use learning program that focuses on a particular topic or skill. All packages comprise a guide for the facilitator/trainer and a workbook for the participants. Some packages are supported with additional media—such as video—or learning aids, instruments, or other devices to help participants understand concepts or practice and develop skills.

- *Facilitator/trainer's guide* Contains an introduction to the program, advice on how to organize and facilitate the learning event, and step-by-step instructor notes. The guide also contains copies of presentation materials—handouts, presentations, and overhead designs, for example—used in the program.
- *Participant's workbook* Contains exercises and reading materials that support the learning goal and serves as a valuable reference and support guide for participants in the weeks and months that follow the learning event. Typically, each participant will require his or her own workbook.

ELECTRONIC CD-ROMs and web-based products transform static Pfeiffer content into dynamic, interactive experiences. Designed to take advantage of the searchability, automation, and ease-of-use that technology provides, our e-products bring convenience and immediate accessibility to your workspace.

METHODOLOGIES

CASE STUDY A presentation, in narrative form, of an actual event that has occurred inside an organization. Case studies are not prescriptive, nor are they used to prove a point; they are designed to develop critical analysis and decision-making skills. A case study has a specific time frame, specifies a sequence of events, is narrative in structure, and contains a plot structure—an issue (what should be/have been done?). Use case studies when the goal is to enable participants to apply previously learned theories to the circumstances in the case, decide what is pertinent, identify the real issues, decide what should have been done, and develop a plan of action.

ENERGIZER A short activity that develops readiness for the next session or learning event. Energizers are most commonly used after a break or lunch to stimulate or refocus the group. Many involve some form of physical activity, so they are a useful way to counter post-lunch lethargy. Other uses include transitioning from one topic to another, where "mental" distancing is important.

EXPERIENTIAL LEARNING ACTIVITY (ELA) A facilitator-led intervention that moves participants through the learning cycle from experience to application (also known as a Structured Experience). ELAs are carefully thought-out designs in which there is a definite learning purpose and intended outcome. Each step—everything that participants do during the activity—facilitates the accomplishment of the stated goal. Each ELA includes complete instructions for facilitating the intervention and a clear statement of goals, suggested group size and timing, materials required, an explanation of the process, and, where appropriate, possible variations to the activity. (For more detail on Experiential Learning Activities, see the Introduction to the *Reference Guide to Handbooks and Annuals*, 1999 edition, Pfeiffer, San Francisco.)

GAME A group activity that has the purpose of fostering team sprit and togetherness in addition to the achievement of a pre-stated goal. Usually contrived—undertaking a desert expedition, for example—this type of learning method offers an engaging means for participants to demonstrate and practice business and interpersonal skills. Games are effective for team building and personal development mainly because the goal is subordinate to the process—the means through which participants reach decisions, collaborate, communicate, and generate trust and understanding. Games often engage teams in "friendly" competition.

ICEBREAKER A (usually) short activity designed to help participants overcome initial anxiety in a training session and/or to acquaint the participants with one another. An icebreaker can be a fun activity or can be tied to specific topics or training goals. While a useful tool in itself, the icebreaker comes into its own in situations where tension or resistance exists within a group.

INSTRUMENT A device used to assess, appraise, evaluate, describe, classify, and summarize various aspects of human behavior. The term used to describe an instrument depends primarily on its format and purpose. These terms include survey, questionnaire, inventory, diagnostic survey, and poll. Some uses of instruments include providing instrumental feedback to group members, studying here-and-now processes or functioning within a group, manipulating group composition, and evaluating outcomes of training and other interventions.

Instruments are popular in the training and HR field because, in general, more growth can occur if an individual is provided with a method for focusing specifically on his or her own behavior. Instruments also are used to obtain information that will serve as a basis for change and to assist in workforce planning efforts.

Paper-and-pencil tests still dominate the instrument landscape with a typical package comprising a facilitator's guide, which offers advice on administering the instrument and interpreting the collected data, and an initial set of instruments. Additional instruments are available separately. Pfeiffer, though, is investing heavily in e-instruments. Electronic instrumentation provides effortless distribution and, for larger groups particularly, offers advantages over paper-and-pencil tests in the time it takes to analyze data and provide feedback.

LECTURETTE A short talk that provides an explanation of a principle, model, or process that is pertinent to the participants' current learning needs. A lecturette is intended to establish a common language bond between the trainer and the participants by providing a mutual frame of reference. Use a lecturette as an introduction to a group activity or event, as an interjection during an event, or as a handout.

MODEL A graphic depiction of a system or process and the relationship among its elements. Models provide a frame of reference and something more tangible, and more easily remembered, than a verbal explanation. They also give participants something to "go on," enabling them to track their own progress as they experience the dynamics, processes, and relationships being depicted in the model.

ROLE PLAY A technique in which people assume a role in a situation/scenario: a customer service rep in an angry-customer exchange, for example. The way in which the role is approached is then discussed and feedback is offered. The role play is often repeated using a different approach and/or incorporating changes made based on feedback received. In other words, role playing is a spontaneous interaction involving realistic behavior under artificial (and safe) conditions.

SIMULATION A methodology for understanding the interrelationships among components of a system or process. Simulations differ from games in that they test or use a model that depicts or mirrors some aspect of reality in form, if not necessarily in content. Learning occurs by studying the effects of change on one or more factors of the model. Simulations are commonly used to test hypotheses about what happens in a system—often referred to as "what if?" analysis—or to examine best-case/worst-case scenarios.

THEORY A presentation of an idea from a conjectural perspective. Theories are useful because they encourage us to examine behavior and phenomena through a different lens.

TOPICS

The twin goals of providing effective and practical solutions for workforce training and organization development and meeting the educational needs of training and human resource professionals shape Pfeiffer's publishing program. Core topics include the following:

Leadership & Management
Communication & Presentation
Coaching & Mentoring
Training & Development
e-Learning
Teams & Collaboration
OD & Strategic Planning
Human Resources
Consulting

What will you find on pfeiffer.com?

- The best in workplace performance solutions for training and HR professionals

- Downloadable training tools, exercises, and content

- Web-exclusive offers

- Training tips, articles, and news

- Seamless on-line ordering

- Author guidelines, information on becoming a Pfeiffer Affiliate, and much more

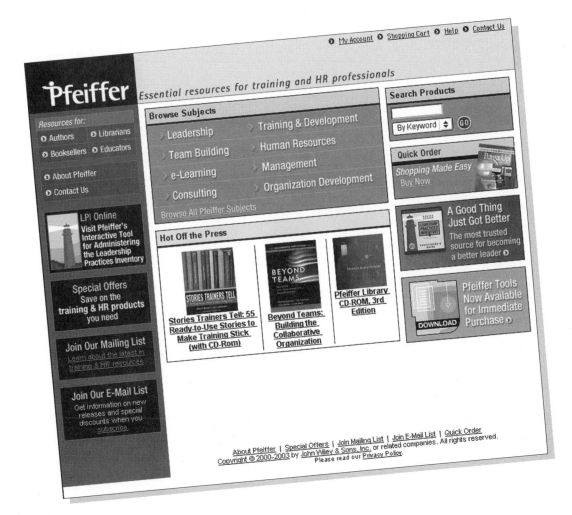

Discover more at www.pfeiffer.com

Customer Care

Have a question, comment, or suggestion? Contact us! We value your feedback and we want to hear from you.

For questions about this or other Pfeiffer products, you may contact us by:

E-mail: **customer@wiley.com**

Mail: **Customer Care Wiley/Pfeiffer**
        10475 Crosspoint Blvd.
        Indianapolis, IN 46256

Phone: **(US) 800-274-4434** (Outside the US: 317-572-3985)

Fax: **(US) 800-569-0443** (Outside the US: 317-572-4002)

To order additional copies of this title or to browse other Pfeiffer products, visit us online at **www.pfeiffer.com**.

For **Technical Support** questions call **(800) 274-4434**.

For authors guidelines, log on to www.pfeiffer.com and click on "Resources for Authors."

If you are . . .

A **college bookstore, a professor, an instructor, or work in higher education** and you'd like to place an order or request an exam copy, please contact jbreview@wiley.com.

A **general retail bookseller** and you'd like to establish an account or speak to a local sales representative, contact Melissa Grecco at 201-748-6267 or mgrecco@wiley.com.

An **exclusively on-line bookseller**, contact Amy Blanchard at 530-756-9456 or ablanchard @wiley.com or Jennifer Johnson at 206-568-3883 or jjohnson@wiley.com, both of our On-line Sales department.

A **librarian or library representative**, contact John Chambers in our Library Sales department at 201-748-6291 or jchamber@wiley.com.

A **reseller, training company/consultant, or corporate trainer**, contact Charles Regan in our Special Sales department at 201-748-6553 or cregan@wiley.com.

A **specialty retail distributor** (includes specialty gift stores, museum shops, and corporate bulk sales), contact Kim Hendrickson in our Special Sales department at 201-748-6037 or khendric@wiley.com.

Purchasing for the **Federal government**, contact Ron Cunningham in our Special Sales department at 317-572-3053 or rcunning@wiley.com.

Purchasing for a **State or Local government**, contact Charles Regan in our Special Sales department at 201-748-6553 or cregan@wiley.com.